PEARLIE GATES

LaQuisha Martin

Relentless Publishing House, LLC

Columbia, SC

Pearlie Gates Copyright © 2019 by LaQuisha Martin.

All rights reserved. Printed in the United States of America. No part of this book may be used or reproduced in any manner whatsoever without written permission except in the case of brief quotations em- bodied in critical articles or reviews.

This book is a work of fiction. Names, characters, businesses, organiza- tions, places, events and incidents either are the product of the author's imagination or are used fictitiously. Any resemblance to actual persons, living or dead, events, or locales is entirely coincidental.

Published by :

Relentless Publishing House, LLC

www.relentlesspublishing.com

ISBN: 9781948829984

First Edition: November 2019

10 9 8 7 6 5 4 3 2 1

TABLE OF CONTENTS

Introduction	2
Chapter One: Fall Fresh	5
Chapter Two: Fell Me Up	13
Chapter Three: Trust In You	23
Chapter Four: You Know My Name	41
Chapter Five: I'm Free	47
Chapter Six: Let It Rain	59
Chapter Seven: Mercy Said No	71
Poem: Let's Close Our Eyes	77
About the Author	86

Let's Close Our Eyes

Can you feel the peace inside of me?
I've closed my eyes and you will never imagine what I see
The clouds family the clouds are so beautiful and white
The feeling is something I will never feel twice...

Introduction

My day-to-day life consists of being a mother, daughter, sister, friend, and social worker. I attend church, and my prayer life is okay, but it could always be better. I enjoy my peace and quiet whenever I can get it. I have been searching for something more, but not sure of what it was. I realized I don't visit home (my hometown Mount Gilead, NC) as much as I did in the past. My son Xavier has many activities that keeps me busy. So, when I can relax, I cherish every minute of it.

When my grandmother Catherine died in 2012, my mom (Bernice) moved to Charlotte to be closer to me, so now I rarely visit my hometown. In my spare time, I read a little, but mostly I find myself writing. Journaling allows me to identify with my thoughts and feelings. Since my grandma's death, I have inwardly held on to so much. I'm still trying to find my way. You see death paralyzed me emotionally and physically since I was a child. I feel like whenever death comes, my family will decide, who is going to tell Keisha. Well, grandma was the one who got us through those storms. She raised my cousins, sisters, and myself as our parents worked in hosiery mills and lumberyards, so this left grandma in charge. We all had our special relationships with grandma, but regardless of the relationship, we all depended upon her the most.

Pearlie Ann Martin is a cousin I grew up with. Her nickname is Kat. When she came home from the hospital, our family immediately called her Kat. This nickname suited her because of her big white glossy eyes, dark beautiful skin, with jet black, silky, and shiny hair. She never gave me a hard time when I had to be in charge. She listened, not always complied, but she did listen. I remember when she had her first and only child. I was in grad-school and working. I left work and came to the hospital. I visited for a while but left early due to an early work schedule. It was an hour upon me leaving that she gave birth to Tykerius (Ty). Since that moment, he has been known as my baby Ty. I'm not sure when I started calling Kat by her name Pearl, but I figured she was too old to be called Kat. We don't see each other much, but the times we do they are priceless. Pearl doesn't speak about her health much, but the family and I can see that her health is declining. She will not reveal to anyone in the family the truth about what's going on with her. I understood because I'm a private person as well. Grandma would say, "Everybody doesn't need to know all your business." The key word is "all" yet knowing "some" is just as important.

I feel something is moving, but I'm not sure what it is. When you are not aware what is coming, God does. When your storm comes, you can decide to do many things. You can run from it, ignore it, fight it, and give up, or you can surrender to God, lean on God's understanding, and allow the Holy Spirit to direct you. For some, they will go through the storm with their own strength (not getting anywhere), but there are others who will surrender to God and allow Him to get them through (God advances, and those individuals are forever changed). Throughout this book, you will see how our story unfolded. God is a mighty God. A God who sits high and looks low. He is a comforter, defender, healer, leader, and so much more.

Through the course of time, you will see how God used me in Pearl's life, how He uses Pearl in my life, but most of all how He advances in us both.

Chapter 1: Fall Fresh

Pearl calls me several times when she is in the hospital. She doesn't call every time, but as time progresses, she calls more frequently. It's September of 2016, the starting point for Pearl and I. I'm sitting at my desk and Pearl comes to my mind. I know she is in Chapel Hill hospital, but I don't know why. I call her to see how she is doing. When she picks up the phone, it's a very low and strange voice,

"Is this Pearl?"
"Hey Keisha, I couldn't recognize your voice either."
"Pearl, I'm just calling to check on you and to make sure you are behaving yourself."

She giggles and then she tells me she is very sick. As she is in the middle of our conversation, she puts the doctor on the phone. I hear someone ask her, "who am I speaking to?" Pearl responds, "this is my cousin LaQuisha, you can speak with her, and she will explain it to me." As the doctor begin speaking to me, I'm in my social worker's mode. I know to write down everything from the doctor's name, contact number, and ask as many questions as I can. After my conversation with the doctor, the phone was returned to Pearl. I explain to Pearl they need to give her some medicine at 11:00pm. It must be at 11:00pm and she agrees. I tell her I love her, and she says the same. I feel nervous and concerned. I wait in my seat in silence. My body is motionless. I place all the information in a notebook and try to continue with my day. The next day while at work, I receive another phone call. It's a resident physician. He is very concerned, due to Pearl refusing the medication. He says, "This is a symptom of her condition, as it alters behaviors and thought process." He asks me to speak with her again. I tell Pearl the importance of the medication, so they can plan for surgery. She repeats back to me what I said to be sure she understands. I want to be sure the doctor is correct about her mental status and it isn't just Pearl been stubborn. Pearl repeats back what I said without a problem and she understands they are there to help. She doesn't want me to call her later to remind her to take the medication. We talk a little while longer, but something happens just before we end the call. It sends chills down my body. I'm frozen with tears in my eyes.

    As Pearl says goodbye, we both say, "I love you." Then there's a laugh from her, it isn't the normal laugh. Can you think of the scariest movie you have watched? You know when the villain laughs after realizing he has fooled everyone. Just imagine that sound coming from someone you love. Can you feel it, that's scary right? I hang up the phone and run to the chaplain. No one is in the office. I'm in the chapel. I'm crying and praying. I cannot get her laugh out of my head. I need to talk with someone, I go to my friend Shay. As tears, roll down my face she realizes this is serious. She tells me to go check on Pearl. I tell her, "You really don't know me, well do you? I'm telling her I'm the one family consoles when something like this happens. I'm the one when bad news come, it takes three or more to tell me. I'm not good at this, I can't do it." She asks if there is anyone else who could go with me, and to call them because we need to go to the hospital immediately. I'm heading to my office as I pray silently. I'm asking God to calm me and tell me who to call. I'm sitting quietly. Something says, "Jeannette, call Jeannette (our cousin)." I pick up the phone and I tell her what's going on. We agree to meet at Chris' (my sister) house and ride together to the hospital. Jeanette explains she will pick up Vanice (Pearl's mom) and update her on Pearl. I'm talking with Bethany, my supervisor, about Pearl. She says without hesitation, "LaQuisha please go, don't worry about here." But I need to do something I have control over because I will face the unknown. When I do, I'm at the mercy of God. I finish my paperwork before I leave.

     As I'm driving to my sister's house, I feel so full on the inside. I need to purge, to let out a big cry. The phone rings and I cut my cry off to answer. I answer the phone, it's Shay. While she is talking, I'm trying to hold back my tears, but I need to release what's inside of me. My stomach hurts holding this in, and I want to be sure I finish before I reach Chris' house. Shay can hear something in my voice. She encourages me to just let it go. I do not want my family to worry about me because Pearl is the focus. As I wipe my tears, hang up with Shay, I turn on my music and Luther Barnes begin to play.

     God is in this moment. I know God is with me and I must trust Him. I realize music calms and consoles me. I will focus on God and not lose sight of Him. As I reach Chris' house, she has so many questions and I can't provide any answers at the time. I need to remain calm and stay in this place with God and keep my feelings under control. I tell her, "I'm not sure, I will let you know when we get there." We head out and I'm driving. Vanice and Jeanette talk for about twenty minutes into the ride, but it gets quiet. I realize we all are scared. So, I turn on relaxing music. It is so soothing. Everyone gets quiet and the ride is smooth and peaceful. Vanice works on crossword puzzles and Jeanette looks out the window. I know our thoughts are the same: "what is really going on with Pearl?"

When we arrive at the hospital, Pearl is cursing like a sailor. Her mouth needs a pop from grandma. We try to talk to her about the medication she needs to take. Then we try not to say anything, so she will calm down, but she continues cursing. We are in complete shock. She does not listen when we tell her to stop with the language. Jeanette says, "okay we are leaving, you are not going to talk to us like this." Pearl immediately apologizes, but we are all so overwhelmed and scared we leave the room. Vanice responds, "I will stay. She wants me to stay." I reply, "No you will not. You are not going to be able to handle this, let's go." Vanice cries, "I have to take her bag in there. What am I going to tell her?" Jeanette grabs the bag. "I will take it. You stay here." It breaks Vanice's heart to see her daughter this way and she is scared. I knew if I left Vanice here, she will call me before the night is over to come back to get her. Vanice asks me if Kat will be okay. I calmly tell her, "The longer Pearl waits to have surgery, the worse she will be. Pearl needs to take the medicine, so they can determine the plan of care".

As we head to the nurse's station, a nurse reassures us Pearl will get the medicine. As we leave, we all know it will be a long and quiet ride home. I'm a mother too. It's our job to take care of our children and when we can't we feel we have failed them. You feel helpless and other times hopeless. During this journey, we must depend more on God than ourselves. We must believe God will direct us as the Holy Spirit guides us. No one speaks another word until we reach Chris' house. Chris wants answers, but I'm so exhausted I'm not able to give her any. I still have another 45 minutes to get home, and I work tomorrow. As tears roll down my face, she says, "Just text when you get home." The drive home is long and quiet. I'm so emotionally drained. I'm in the drive way and not sure how I got here. I'm sitting in the car thinking "Grandma (Ma) would know what to do, but she isn't here anymore." I want to know God's plans? We are still grieving over grandma. Lord, what can we do? What should we do?

    The next day, I'm going through my regular routine and I feel physically beaten up. I get up and pray. I get ready for work as Xavier gets ready for school. Later, I'm at my desk, but not sure when the phone will ring. I want to stay seated because I'm so afraid to miss the call. As I pray at my desk, I know when it is time, the call will come. As the day progresses the resident calls and states, "She took the medicine, but it is worse than the doctors expected. They want to perform surgery the first day of next week." I advise him to call her mother to schedule the surgery. The resident wants me to make the decision. He says, "Pearlie wants you to make this decision." I inform the resident, "If there is no health care power of attorney or living will with my name on it, her mother and father are next in line to make these decisions." The resident understands and calls Vanice. He immediately calls me back because her number is disconnected. I feel the weight of the world on my shoulders. My mom and I try to contact Vanice, but we are unable to reach her. I am her emergency contact, so I give consent for Pearl to have surgery.

    I have a self-talk to remind myself it is not time to be afraid. There are more important things to do. I call Jeanette to let her know surgery is scheduled for September 20th and I need for her to come with me, I need her support. She agrees. As I call Pearl's brothers, James and Jerry, I tell them they need to be there with us to support Vanice. I call Tasha (our cousin), and she agrees to be there as well. Pearl and Tasha are like sisters. Vanice informs me that Tykerius does not want to be there. He is only 18 and I can understand. The concern is the weekend. Boy, it is hell. I receive call after call from the nurses. Pearl is upset after every phone call. I cannot figure out who she is talking to. I can't monitor her phone calls, so I request for them to move the phone out of her reach. I also request a sign on the door stating, "No visitors!" No one can call her room unless they know the password. I'm trying to keep her as calm as possible.

By Monday morning, I am emotionally and mentally exhausted. Tuesday morning, Jeanette, Tasha, Vanice, James, Jerry, and I travel to Chapel Hill. James and Jerry are finally asleep after forty-five minutes into the ride. They argue over every little thing, but we all know it's the nervousness. It is very comical. If one breathes louder than the other, the other will say it is too loud. If one has a Reese's cup and the other does not, Vanice gives the other one. They are asleep now that their stomachs are full. Vanice and I are in the backseats. She asks me what do I have to read, I hand her my daily devotional book and she begins to read quietly. The windows are down, and the breeze is crisp and cool, which is a very relaxing mood. In quietness, you can hear God the most and the rest of the ride the Holy Spirit gives us comfort. When we arrive, the nurse tells us Pearl's surgery will start soon. We rush to her side. Pearl is scared, and we understand. Tasha talks to her as the doctors asks for consent. Pearl quickly responds, "Keisha sign the papers." I sign the papers as she looks at me. I tell her to behave herself and try not to worry. She replies in the voice that I recognize, "Okay Keisha." Pearl never argued with me. She doesn't always listen to what I say but she never argues.

We all tell Pearl we love her, and we all head to the waiting room. The surgery takes about ten hours. We watch TV, complete crossword puzzles, while others are on their phones. Jeanette is knitting, however, I'm not sure what I'm doing exactly. Finally, the nurse calls us into the consult room. The doctors talk from exhaustion, as we listen with the same exhaustion. Two by two we enter Pearl's room as Jeanette walks in with me, Pearl's eyes are swollen so much she can barely close them. She worries about Ty and we are assuring her he is fine. Pearl talks a little more, but falls asleep minutes after. Jeanette and I look at each other. No words are spoken but concerns are present. We visit with her for a little while longer as we prepare to leave.

If you want God to laugh, tell Him your plans. In my mind, the next day will be quiet and I will get some rest. Well Pearl has something else in mind. The nurse calls and says Pearlie is aggressive (physically and verbally). I'm standing in my dining room scratching my head and saying to myself "I thought she had major surgery." I'm so sleep deprived I'm not sure if this is a dream or not. It isn't a dream and Pearl is showing out big time. The nurse and I figure out a plan and change the nurse to a more seasoned and experienced nurse. Thursday, I'm back to work and my phone rings, it's my baby sister Nikki. I'm thinking "Pearl what are you up to now," but it isn't about Pearl. Nikki's voice is too calm. You know when someone is so scared, their voice is still as they speak. I can hear this in her voice. I know something is terribly wrong. To my surprise, it isn't about Pearl. This time it's about Nikki and her unborn daughter, my niece Uriah. As she gives me the news, I proceed to my car and begin driving to the hospital. As I'm in route to the hospital to be with Nikki, I receive a call from Vanice. Pearl wants to come home, but I'm so shocked because she just had major surgery. I'm thinking she will be tired and sedated, but I was wrong. I call Pearl, and it is a struggle to get her to understand it's best she remains in the hospital. She wants to come home, but the doctors recommend other options. Pearl shows her butt for real. She curses out the social worker at the center over the phone and they are refusing to take her. The hospital staff is so upset about her behavior, they discharge her. I call to speak with the physician to see if these are symptoms of the surgery, but Pearl is cleared to make her own decisions. So, nope it's all Pearl. She wants to go home, and she is doing everything she can to get there. I'm no longer able to make the decisions. Pearl isn't arguing with me, but she isn't agreeing with me either. I feel it is a bad idea for her to go home, but I can't do anything. I don't know what more to do with her or for her. I know I must take care of my sister, Nikki. After Pearl returns home, the family is so disappointed in her, but no one can get her to do what the doctors say. So, she heals, and we continue to live life as we know it. Pearl calls from time to time, and whenever I visit during holidays, I get a chance to see her. Again, if you want God to laugh tell Him your plans. It's another year and God was preparing me last year for something more. Come along with me on this journey with Pearl.

Chapter Two: Fill Me Up

Friday, March 31, 2017, I am driving back from Virginia Tech University. Xavier and I went for a tour. My sister Chris is calling. She is telling me Pearl is being transferred to CMC main in Charlotte. I'm asking Chris what happen, but she is not sure. Chris tells me that Vanice is coming with Pearl. We are discussing if it is critical, however, Vanice did not say. I begin checking my phone, and no missed calls from her. So, we will just wait and see. As I'm driving, I'm thinking of all the other things I have going on for the weekend. I know I will not be able to visit Pearl until Sunday. Xavier and I are taking our time getting back to the house. It's raining and I'm not too comfortable driving down from the mountains in the rain. It's about six o'clock pm and we are tired.

    As I am getting ready to relax, I remember Xavier has basketball practice for three hours tomorrow. I have cleaning, grocery shopping, and other things to do tomorrow. By the time I close my eyes, its already Saturday morning. I'm running around trying to complete my numerous amounts of tasks for today. I notice it's time to get Xavier to practice. I'm thinking I'm late, but the coach isn't here. We have been waiting outside for twenty minutes. I'm thinking, "Lord, I could really be home right now resting." Finally, everyone arrives. Xavier and the boys are practicing and I'm introducing myself to the other parents. This is Xavier's first year with this team. I'm looking down at my phone. No one calls all day about Pearl. That's a good sign. So, I'm going to get out of my own head and watch my son practice. Xavier is finally finished with practice and we are picking up dinner and heading to the house to chill for the rest of the day. My plan is to shower, put on my comfortable clothes, and watch television. As I'm watching TV, my phone rings. It's 10:30pm. It's Tasha. "Keisha can you go check on Kat she said she can't breathe?" "Tasha it's 10:30. I think visiting hours may be over, but I will call." I call the hospital and they connect me to the nurse's station. "My name is LaQuisha. I'm a social worker with CMC (I figured it can't hurt) and my cousin Pearlie Martin says she can't breathe. Can you check on her please?" The nurse goes in and repositions her. I call Pearl and she is crying. She wants to come home. I'm trying to get her to calm down. Pearl thinks the nurses are trying to hurt her. I'm trying to reassure her she will be fine. "Pearl, take some deep breaths for me and try to relax." It's taking me some time to get her to focus on me and not what's going on around her, but thank God, she is calming down. I am able to get off the phone with Pearl to call Tasha. "Pearl is sleeping. The nurse checked in on her and I will go see her tomorrow." Tasha sighs with relief and ends our call with "I love you."

    Sunday morning, Xavier and I are in church and the service is great. We arrive at home and I'm putting on dinner for today and for next week. I look at the clock and I realize I need to go to the hospital. I'm hesitant about going. I don't want to go back and forth with Pearl today about staying in the hospital.

As I'm pulling into a parking space in the parking deck, I see familiar faces. It is Tasha, Vanice, Tasha's daughter, Tykayla and her boyfriend Stanley. We all walk in together. As we approach the elevators, Vanice states, "She is in ICU." I'm looking at Vanice wondering when did this happen? Now, I'm thinking to myself, "Why didn't I realize this last night when I spoke with the nurse?" We are getting off the elevator and head towards her room, I pause. Something just does not seem right. I feel like something is wrong. We are walking in and I see death. I run out of the room to the nursing station. "Excuse me, why does Pearl look like that? Her eyes are dark yellow and glossy, her breathing is heavy, and she looks swollen!" The nurse says, "I thought this was her baseline?" "NO ma'am this is not her baseline. Tell me what's going on with my cousin!" Another nurse enters the conversation and says, "Pearlie is declining, and we don't know why. Do you know anything?" I'm thinking what happened and how long had this been going on? Was she like this when they transferred her over here? As the nurses are standing here looking at me, I'm frozen. Vanice comes out the room crying. "She did not look like that when I left her on Friday. She looks bad, Keisha something is wrong." Tasha is standing in the room along with Stanley and Tykayla. I'm thinking to myself, "We need to take a moment. We need to step out." I'm not sure if I'm speaking the words out loud. I'm watching Tasha, Stanley, and Tykayla come out of the room. Am I talking to them? I realize I'm not talking aloud. They are just doing what I am thinking.

    As we sit in the waiting room trying to figure out what's happening, no one wants to go back into Pearl's room. You can see the fear in our eyes and on our faces. Tasha is the first to speak, "I need to take her phone back in there, but I don't want to." Tasha looks at Vanice as she is shaking her head no. I tell everyone I don't want to go in there either." So, we are sitting here quietly and in disbelief. Finally, I stand and say, "Okay, I will go take the phone in there, but I don't think she needs a phone." No one is saying a word. I begin walking slowly, my head is hurting, my heart is racing, and mouth dry as a bone. I'm getting closer to the room, and I feel like my heart is going to pop out of my chest. "Lord, please help me, Lord please help Pearl." I'm in the doorway, and I pause. Pearl's back is facing me, I hear Pearl talking. I'm looking in the room and I don't see anyone. I know she is not on the phone because I have it in my hand. Who is Pearl talking to? She is having a full conversation and it is freaking me out. I walk over to her and she looks up at me and softly says, "Keisha give me some of this water." The nurse comes in and says, "she can't have anything to eat or drink because she needs to have test, she can have some ice chips. I will go get her some." As the nurse leaves, Pearl says again, "Keisha give me some of this water." I tell her, "That's not water. The nurse is going to bring you some ice chips." Pearl says with a soft slow voice, "No, here is the water, give me some of this water." My eyes are big, I take a breath in as I'm looking at Pearl holding up her IV line. Tears are rolling down my face. I reply, that's your IV, Pearl the nurse is going to bring you some ice chips," As she looks at me with those big beautiful eyes she says, "What's wrong, I'm going to be okay Keisha." She turns her head as if my tears are getting on her last nerve. I realize she can't see what I see. She does not feel what I feel. Does she know I see death? I can't hold back my tears because I know what the Holy Spirit is saying to me. Did I say it to her, of course not? I look up, Tasha is standing in the doorway. She comes over and whispers in my ear, "You got to be strong, you can't cry." I nod okay, but I can't hold back my tears anymore. I need to cry because it's hurting me physically. I need to do what makes me feel better and that is to cry. But I stop, it's not about me. The nurse enters, Tasha and I move back, and I whisper in Tasha's ear "She doesn't look good Tasha something is wrong." Tasha nods in agreement and says, "I know." As the nurse steps back to where we are standing, Tasha moves to Pearl's side. The nurse asks if we know anything else about her medical history? I told her I didn't, but to call Pinehurst Hospital as they may have more information. Then I hear Pearl say to Tasha, "They said I don't look right. They said I'm not going to make it." Tasha asks, "Who said that?" Pearl closes her eyes and does not respond. Tasha and I are looking at each other frighten and helpless. I'm wondering who are "they?" Did she hear us, no way she couldn't hear us because it was a whisper and the machines are loud? Who are "they?" These are just the many questions going through my mind as Tasha and I stand facing each other. I motion for Tasha to leave the room. We are in the hallway and are looking back at Pearl. She is asleep. The nurse approaches us explaining that the test will take a little time and she can call us with an update. I check with the nurse to see whose contact information is listed on Pearl's paperwork. Pearl has me down as her emergency contact, but they also have Vanice's number. Tasha and I are walking down the hall quietly and slowly. I feel like I'm dreaming, walking in quick sand, and unfamiliar with what I just saw. We approach the waiting room, but we have no updates to share. I say to Vanice, "Let's go home and give her some time to rest. They will call with an update". We are walking out together, but we are all speechless. They have an hour and half drive back to Mount Gilead. I have only fifteen minutes, but it all feels the same.

My drive home is quiet no music, no phone calls, nothing. "Lord, I'm not sure what you have planned, but please help Pearl." I arrive home and I'm standing in my living room. I grab my phone to call Tykerius. As the phone is ringing, "Lord please guide my words." I hear "Hello?" The voice is deep, a man's voice. I pause for a moment. "Ty, is this you?" "Yea, it's me, hey Keisha." "My baby Ty, I need to talk with you. It's about your mom." He replies, "What's wrong? She's trying to come home again isn't she?" "No, baby, she is sick, and you really need to go see her." There is silence on the phone, and he replies, "Yes ma'am I will be there I will need to find a ride." He hangs up the phone. You see, Ty is in Asheboro, NC with Pearl's dad and family. I'm not sure who knows she is in Charlotte, but I know they don't know how she is right now. I'm standing in my kitchen looking at the phone and trying to figure out why my head is pounding. I'm getting water from the sink, starring at the window. My mind is wondering, "Is this really happening, what is it, what is about to happen?" As I walk over to the sofa, I envision I am in a black dress and I am fixing Vanice's hair. I begin to feel uneasy as my heart is racing. Then I hear a phone ring. I jump up looking around for my phone. I locate my phone. My voice trembling as I say, "hello?" It is Vanice. She is talking fast and screaming at the same time. She yells, "Keisha how fast can you get to the hospital they just put Kat on a breathing machine?" I immediately respond, "Ten minutes oh God, what is going on?" I'm up trying to find my keys. I'm not sure if I hung up on Vanice or not. As I run and get in the car I yell to Xavier "I will be right back." He doesn't need to know right now. I'm trying to get there and as I'm driving, I'm praying. I'm crying and I'm praying. Then the tears stop. All I can do is pray.

I'm running up to the ICU to her room and they are working on

Pearl. There are so many in her room, the machines, nurses in and out talking about "what" I have no clue. I look around and although there are many people here, I've never felt so alone in my life. "Lord, you know I'm not the strong one why am I here by myself?" I call Jeanette, "Get over here right now, I can't do this by myself. I just can't, she is on a breathing machine!" Jeanette replies, "WHAT, oh my God, what happened?" "I don't know. Just get over here right now!" As I'm still standing out in the hallway and the nurses and doctors continue to work on Pearl. "Lord it's me, please help her, please help us. What should I do? Lord please HELP!" A nurse comes to tell me, "We lowered her bed to give her some medication and she stopped breathing." I can't hear anything after that. The nurse's mouth is still moving but I feel like I'm being brought into the center of a tornado. I'm looking at my 33-year old cousin on life support. I'm looking at what the Holy Spirit revealed to me just two hours ago. I am looking at death. I'm crying wanting to know what she wants me to do. "Lord, God, I'm not sure if she wants this. Lord, I don't know what to do." The phone rings and it's Tasha. "Keisha, we are on the way. It's me, Vanice, James, and Jerry. How is she?" I tell her to, "drive safely but it's not good." I hang up the phone, I begin to cry once more. "Lord, this is not what I do. I can't do this. Look at her, Lord please." As I'm trying to calm myself down, I continue to pray aloud. "Lord I need you because I don't know what I'm doing here out of all people in the family, you chose me to be here. Jesus help please Jesus!" As I place my head on Pearl's head, my voice is soft as I speak, "What do you want me to do?" I wipe my tears and the nurse enters the room. She asks, "Do you need anything, can I call anyone?" "My family is on the way, but I need for you to let me handle them. Our family can be loud and hard to control. They are loving but seeing her like this is going to be overwhelming." The nurse understands, "Yes ma'am what do you need?" I request that the doctor tells them what happened, but to do it in the waiting room because if they see her first, they will not be able to process anything the doctor is saying. She agrees, "let me know when they arrive."

I call Tasha and tell her, "When you get here go to the waiting room and I will come out." Tasha says with hesitation "Okay, but Keisha, is she?" There is a pause and I know what the pause means. I explained, "Just go to the waiting room okay." Since I'm not crying, I feel it brings Tasha some comfort. If I'm holding it together, it will help them to focus on the road and arrive safely. As I'm waiting on them, I can only look at Pearl and ponder. I can recall the times we laughed, played, cried together. How did we get here? How did we get to this place? When Tasha arrives, she calls and asks if she can come back. I don't see the nurse, so I tell her, "Just you okay but wait at the nursing station." Little did I know Tasha is heading to the room as she is talking to me, but the nurse stops her. As I'm walking out, it is all four of them Tasha, James, Jerry, and Vanice. I quickly tell them, "I need for you to go back to the waiting room, so the doctor can talk to everyone." Jerry blurts out, "She's dead oh Lord." Then Vanice crys "Oh no!" Tasha shakes her head and say, "No Keisha no!" James loudly tells everyone, "Y'all shut up and let her talk!" I calmly respond to everyone, "No she is not, she is on a breathing machine. Please let's go to the waiting room and wait for the doctor to tell us what is going on." The nurse and doctor come in to speak with us. I step out to tell another nurse what I need to do. I tell the nurse, "Let me lead all of them back to her room. I will direct them to be sure only two at a time goes in to visit. This will give them the time, they need." She agrees, "Okay." I move over and start to pray. "Lord, I need for you to direct my path allow the Holy Spirit to guide me and fill this place with your love, peace, and understanding. Lord I can't do this alone. I need you to speak for me and think for me. You do what you need to do so that I can be what you want me to be. I can't do it by myself. Lord strengthen me where I'm weak, and build me up where I'm torn down in Jesus name." Family from both sides are coming, two at a time they say their goodbyes. It is the most peaceful and loving environment I've ever witnessed. God did what He said he would do. After the visits we all go home. Pearl is a full code and we will wait to see what the doctors say tomorrow. I will continue to pray and ask God for direction. I feel like He is not finish with me or Pearl. There is something else, He wants me to do. I feel it, but I can't figure it out. I'm praying to receive my instructions from the Lord.

*I've closed my eyes and the song is loud and clear
I can feel Him family, I feel His presence here
He makes no mistakes, trust in Him and you will see
This is why I ask, please don't grieve for me*

Chapter Three: Trust In You

I believe I am in a place where God is calling for me to complete a task. I'm not sure what the task is but I know with everything in my body it is going to change my life forever. I know I am waiting for God's direction. All of this seems like an out of body experience. I feel like I am floating, looking around and everything is appearing to be moving in slow motion. My heart is pounding, voices seems distant, I am present, but I feel so far away. Have you ever been in this place?

    I'm driving home from the hospital and Vanice is in the car talking a mile a minute. I can't hear what she is saying, my responses are "okay and umm". I call mom to let her know about Pearl and ask her to meet me at my house. I feel the need to spend time with God and I can't do that if Vanice is here. I can't because my focus will be on Vanice and not on God and Pearl. I need quietness so I can connect with God better. I need space, I need to breathe. I need to get out of my head and listen for a soft still voice. Mom is in the house as Vanice and I pull into the driveway. I want to answer all of mom's questions, but right now I just don't feel well and I'm totally exhausted. I'm telling mom Pearl is on life support and the next 24 to 48 hours are critical. I give her a "look" and she knows what that look is for. You know the "look." You have seen it before. For mom and I, it's the same look I gave her when we found my uncle, her brother Poboy dead in his bed. It is the look she gave me when there was nothing that could be done for grandma. It is the look that tells you that death is here and we can't stop what God has in motion. Mom decides to leave as she hugs me and tells me "I love you baby, try to get some rest." Vanice comes to me and say, 'Love you LaQuisha and thank you." I'm thinking not to tell Xavier right now, I will see how I feel in the morning. The rest of the night I'm crying and rocking myself to sleep. I'm in shock and disbelief, but I know I had no time to sit in it. I know once morning comes, the process will begin again.

    I open my eyes, scanning the room. I'm trying to figure out if I am dreaming or not. I slowly sit up in my bed, turn my body to place my feet on the floor. I'm sitting on the edge of my bed, I'm thinking and for a second Pearl is not on a breathing machine in my mind. Then I hold my head upward and reality seems to slap me in my face. As I'm standing, I decide not to go into work. I call my supervisor Bethany to update her. She asks, "is this the same cousin from last year who had the surgery?" I paused slightly. I forgot Pearl had major surgery seven months ago. I pause because the Holy Spirit is reminding me God was preparing me then for this moment. I pause because this just became real. I say, "yes ma'am, it's Pearl." Bethany pauses and says, "LaQuisha take your time and keep me posted. Is there anything I can do?" I'm standing looking at the wall. I'm listening to her, but I can't really hear her. Still I say, "no not now, but thank you." Bethany knows I am a very private person, so I don't say please don't share this with anyone right now. I'm walking to the restroom to wash my face and hands. I'm looking at myself in the mirror. The person I see in the mirror, is not how I feel at this moment. The person looking back is strong. The person looking back has been through some hard times and knows those times strengthened her for this moment. The person looking back has battle scars, but it's the scars I see that helps me to know she survived. I go into Xavier's room to wake him up. I'm waiting for him to get ready for school and eat before I talk with him about Pearl. As I wait for him to get ready, I ask the Holy Spirit to guide my words in telling him about Pearl. Xavier is all set for school and he is standing in front of me in the living room. "Son, I need to talk with you." As I'm talking, I can't recall what I'm saying. I see Xavier's eyes fill with tears, the look of confusion upon his face. I see Xavier drops his head and then I hear "Oh God no." Xavier replies, "Will she be okay mom? How is Vanice, what about Ty?" "Xavier, son, they are holding on, it is hard to understand right now. We are not sure what is going to happen." Xavier and I are sitting in the living room in complete quietness. He just heard the news, I'm giving him some time to process this. I'm not sure if I have processed it. I ask Xavier, "Do you want to go to school? I'm going over to the hospital to check on Pearl." Xavier slowly responds with a voice of an innocent child says, "yes ma'am I will go to school." As we stand for prayer, the tears are falling from our eyes. We stand praying with Pearl, Ty, and Vanice in our hearts. I'm driving Xavier to school and I say, "Son if you get here and you can't stay, call grandma or me. I don't want you to hold any feelings inside, it's okay to cry, to be upset, to ask questions, to feel whatever you are feeling, but don't hold it in Xavier." He is looking out the window, but he responds slowly, "yes ma'am." We say our "I love you's" before he gets out the car. I look back as I'm driving off like I always do to be sure he doesn't need me.

I'm heading over to the hospital, I feel numb at times. My head feels swimmy, but I'm focusing on the bigger picture. I'm approaching the nurse's station and the nurse from last night is here. She tells me there are no changes and the doctors are heading in to assess her in a few minutes. I go over to Pearl and I still can't believe what I'm seeing. I grab a wet wash cloth to wipe her face and mouth, no response. I let her know I'm here, no response. The doctors enter the room and the news isn't good. They don't know what is going on, they don't know what is causing this to happen. What they do know is her organs are in danger of failing. As I'm standing here with tears in my eyes, I see a face I recognize. It is Dr. Rhonnie Song a resident physician I work with at the doctor's office. She is looking at me with an angelic face, but it's something about her expression also. I can't gather why she is looking at me in this way. Dr. Song is walking towards me and says, "LaQuisha how do you know Pearlie?" "She is my cousin." Tears begin falling from my face. Now I know why her look is different. I'm not a social worker right now, I'm a family member. I'm a family member of a patient who is on life support. I'm the one who is needing assistance, I'm not giving assistance. This is unfamiliar to me, this place, this feeling, this need. Dr. Song asks, "Can I call anyone at the job?" "No, I will be fine." She gives me a hug, and for a small frame woman it is strong and powerful.

The doctors leave the room and I'm here with Pearl once

again by myself. I'm not afraid. I'm not sure what to feel at this moment. I'm just looking at her wondering if she can hear me. "Pearl, tell me what to do? What do you want me to do Pearly Pearl?" No response, I'm just going to sit for a little while. I'm not sure why, but I need to just sit and look at her. The phone rings and it's Vanice. "Keisha, I'm at your house with your mama and your son. I want to see Kat." "I will come get you. Ask mom if she wants to come too?" Vanice tells me, "I have you on speaker phone, she is shaking her head no. Zay-Zay (Xavier's nickname) wants to come." "I will talk with you all when I get there." I'm thinking, I'm not sure if Xavier needs to see Pearl this way. "Lord, guide me with this, he is my son. Tell me what to do." I'm pulling up and they are all standing in the driveway: Xavier, mom, and Vanice. Vanice is chasing Xavier around in circles. Xavier is trying to keep Vanice's mind off Pearl the way he knows how to do. Laughter is good for the soul and if Xavier can help Vanice find laughter or a smile right now, it's God's confirmation to let Xavier go. I pull Xavier aside and say, "Son, Pearl is on machines, she can't speak, I'm not sure if she can hear, but she looks different. Are you sure this is what you want to do?" Xavier looks me in my eyes and says, "Yes ma'am." Mom gives me a kiss on the cheek and whispers, "Keep me posted God bless you baby." We head back to the hospital. Xavier is pushing on Vanice from the back seat. Vanice giggles and say, "Zay-Zay you love me don't you boy?" Xavier smiles, "nope" and giggles. It is very welcoming to hear the giggles, laughter because once we enter this hospital, it will change. We arrive, and the nurse says, "You just left, back already?" "Yes, ma'am this is Pearl's mom Vanice and my son Xavier," Vanice and Xavier enter the room and they both are at her bed side. Vanice and Xavier are telling Pearl "We're here just rest." They sit and watch her monitors and then Xavier starts to tell Vanice what the monitors are and what they are for. I'm smiling, seeing Xavier show compassion and love for his great aunt is a loving moment to witness. We only stay for a little while, there really isn't anything we can do but wait. The drive home is quiet. It's hard to take it all in seeing Pearl like this. Vanice needs to go back home to get clothes and I will continue being the contact person for now. I will visit as much as I can.

    Later, Xavier and I are sitting on the sofa and I want to know how he is feeling. Xavier says, "It's hard to see Kat like that, but we have to give it to God." "You are right son, I just want to be sure you are okay." "I'm good mom, I'm good." The next morning, I drop off Xavier at school and I head to the hospital before I go to work. There are no changes. The doctors are still running test and still not sure what is causing Pearl to decline. I'm at her bedside talking with her. I decide to turn on Pandora. I'm thinking gospel music, good idea. While the music is playing, I'm crying. I know it will help her. I look at the clock and it's time for me to head to work. I tell Pearl "I love you and I'm going to change the music." I'm thinking classical music or relaxation music. I click on the classical station and I laugh. I'm laughing because I can hear Pearl saying to me "Keisha what in the hell you got me listening to." I really can hear her in my ear. It's the funniest thing. I give a kiss goodbye and head to work.

    I'm in my office working. There is a knock at the door. It's a coworker, Miss V coming to tell me "Thank you" for the hard work I do as a social worker and hands me a gift. She is standing with me as I open it. It's a journal. I have a lump in my throat as I'm smiling and thanking her for the thoughtful gift. As she walks out the door, my eyes fill with tears. The last time I received a journal my grandmother died. The person at that time gave me the journal and said, "I know you like to write, and I thought you would like this to help you through your grief." Is this the Holy Spirit speaking? Pearl is in the ICU. She has a long way to go. "Lord are you telling me something?" I figure this will be a good time to start writing. It's amazing how when you enjoy something you can spend hours at it and not realize it. I look at the clock, it's been two hours. Wow, I have a lot on my mind and heart. I'm not up to eating, I decide to go to the chapel for my lunch. It's quiet, I will have a moment to just be. It is a great moment, but too quiet. I open my eyes to realize I fell asleep sitting upright in a chair. I head back to the office, checking my phone to be sure no messages or missed calls. My day seems to be going by I decide I will head to the hospital once I finish up here in the office. As I'm driving over to the hospital, I'm feeling strange. I'm not sure what it is, fatigue, stress, heartache all three and above? I ignore it as I enter the parking deck of the hospital. They are changing shifts so I'm not able to go in. Something says, "Use your badge" and it works I walk right on in. The nurses are speaking as I'm walking by the nursing station. I walk in the room and here is a face I haven't seen before. "How are you?" I say to the nurse who is assessing Pearl. The nurse smiles and says, "You must be Pearlie's cousin the nurse from the previous shift told me you will be stopping by? How was work today?" I'm looking at Pearl but glance back up at the nurse and say, "It was work. How is she doing?" "Still no changes, I know you came this morning, so everything is the same as when you left. We all think the music is nice and inviting when we enter the room." She exits the room and I pull up a chair. I hear the music playing in the back ground. I say to Pearl, "Okay, I will give you a break from this, lets watch some

TV." I search through the channels and I don't see anything that I like. I go over and turn down the lights and sit in the chair and relax. Apparently, I took a nap, the nurse comes in and my eyes open. She smiles and walks back out. I look at the clock I need to get to the house. "Pearl, I'm going to check on Xavier and get some sleep. I will come back in the morning. You get your rest, I love you." I stop by the nursing station to ask if they will have a chaplain and healing hands come to see Pearl? The nurse smiles, tilts her head and says, "Yes ma'am, get some rest and we will see you in the morning." I smile and head out. I'm not sure what more to do other than to pray, but I know Pearl needs all positive energy around her. The chaplain and the healing hands will help. I realize, it's been a long day as I'm walking to my car. I need to let the family know there hasn't been any changes. I don't want to talk to everyone and say repeatedly "there are no changes." I decide to send a group text and it works. Everyone responses and the ones I don't have the numbers for someone will let them know. I'm going home, check on my son, take a shower, and go to bed.

The week seems slow in some moments and fast in others. I realize Dr. Song is here most of the times during rounds, she gives me a small, gentle smile as her head leans to the side. Most times she gives me a hug and asks if there is anyone she can call. Again, I am not the social worker, I am truly out of my element. When life weighs on your shoulders, you try to apply all you have or know to help you through. These are the moments I use my social worker's experience to speak with physicians and nurses, but when I need to just be a family member I am lost. In these moments of solitude when I need something to help me through, God sends me Dr. Song. She does not realize how important she is to me. I am not alone when the doctors come for their rounds because Dr. Song is present. She doesn't say anything, but she is here. As I listen round after round, often not able to comprehend what the doctors are saying, I look at her through eyes of exhaustion. It is the small gentle smile, her warm eyes but most of all the peace she displays. It truly helps during the "moments I am a Family Member." She expresses a sense of compassion and empathy that brings comfort and peace, it's the Holy Spirit speaking through her.

      Well, the weekend is here, and I need to get Xavier to his basketball activities. Vanice and other people are coming to stay with Pearl at the hospital. I'm thinking back over the week. The weekend is going by so fast. I'm cleaning, washing, fixing food for the week. Xavier is a busy young man, but it's good to get out of the house. I enjoy watching Xavier play ball. The excitement seeing him do what he loves brings joy to me. I'm cheering for him, laughing, talking with other parents. This feels good. We are saying our goodbyes to the team and the messages are coming in my phone one after another. I realize for a couple of hours, I forgot Pearl is on a life support. For a couple of hours, I'm living life as I always have. I didn't read the messages right away. I'm telling Xavier how great he was on the basketball court. "Boy, you did your thing back there, I'm proud of you." He smiles and says, "Thank you." Xavier is exhausted. He gets in the car, grabs his water, puts the seat back, takes his shoes off, and relaxes the entire ride home. Xavier gets in the shower and I check my messages. Everyone thinks I'm at the hospital and they want an update. I text to let them all know Vanice is there. I decide not to call Vanice because I want her to have her moment with Pearl and I know others are calling repeatedly. So, I will try to relax and finish my weekend.

Monday morning, I'm in my office. I'm staying busy, Vanice is still at the hospital but leaving today. I need to update my supervisor, but I don't want anyone to see me so I'm walking the long way around. I enter her office and Bethany says, "Hello ma'am, how are you? How is Pearl?" "She is the same, her mom came over this weekend to give me a little break. I will go back to the hospital tonight after work." "LaQuisha you are there for your family, but I think you should talk to a friend. I think this will be helpful for you." At first, I'm thinking why is she telling me this, but then I realize maybe she see what I can't right now. She is looking out for me because my focus is on Pearl and my family. "I will be fine, I will talk with someone. Thank you, Bethany." I'm walking out her door and my eyes are filling with tears. I'm walking back the way I came. I will stop by Shay's office and talk. I reach her door and she is not here. I text Shay and she is in a meeting. I'm walking back towards Bethany's office tears are in my eyes and I'm trying to tilt my head back, so they won't fall. "God, I need to know what to do." I'm not sure why I'm in the lab, but I am. I hear, "Hey are you okay." It's Joann (I call her Jo). Jo is the lab technician and a friend. I turn away from her quickly and say, "I'm fine." As I'm walking quickly to my office with my head down, I close my door and she slides in through a small space just before I close the door. She says, "Just tell me if your son is okay." I nod yes, but the tears are falling. This is not what I want right now, where are these tears coming from? She hugs me and I'm telling her about Pearl. Through my tears, through the crying I am telling her about my 33 year old cousin in the ICU on a breathing machine. Jo looks at me and says, "God wants me to tell you to be strong for your family. He knows you are stronger than what you think. I know this is God talking through me Mountains." (Jo calls me "mountains" because I'm top heavy). Jo is allowing the Holy Spirit to use her. She is delivering a message God needs for me to hear. In the moment God gives his messages through two different people. I decide to stay in my office for the rest of the day. Later, I head over to the hospital and a nurse says, "Hey, I missed you over the weekend. I got a chance to meet some of your family. Did they tell you the doctors are going to take Pearlie off sedation tomorrow? I'm standing here watching her lips move and I'm not sure what this means, but I can't speak. Why can't I speak and why can't I hear what she is saying. It's like I'm watching a movie on mute. I nod and say, "Thank you." I'm walking in her room but still I'm not sure why I'm not asking questions. I'm smiling as I look down at Pearl. I place my head on her head and say, "You're coming back to us. You needed rest and now you are coming back to us." I wash her face as I watch TV. An hour later, I give her a kiss goodbye, turn off the TV, and turn on the Pandora relaxation station. I say my goodbyes to the nurse and head home.

Tuesday evening, I receive a call from the nurse "The doctors decided this morning to take Pearlie off sedation, but she will remain on the vent. She is communicating by hand gestures." I text the family to let them know. I drive over to the hospital. I'm smiling as I enter her room. She turns to me and I say, "Well look at you. I'm glad to see your eyes open." Pearl is trying to talk, and she looks down to her hands. As I follow her eyes, I see restraints. In my mind, I know Pearl is trying to pull the tube out and they place the restrains on to stop her. "Pearl, I will be right back." I go to the nursing station and the nurse says, "We had to put the restraints on because she wants the tube out, but she is not ready yet. She will have test tomorrow to see how she can do without the support of the vent. It may take a few days, but we never know." I tell the nurse, "Thank you" and head back into the room. "Pearl, they will keep this in until you are able to breath on your own." Pearl is shaking her head no. Pearl is trying to say she can breathe without the machine. Pearl and I are going back and forth until I say, "STOP! They are not going to remove it right now, so calm down." Pearl closes her eyes for a second, a tear rolls down the side of her eye and she shakes her head "Yes." I pull up a chair and we are watching TV. She is raising her head up and keeps motioning with her eyes to look at the sink. I spend ten minutes playing twenty questions with Pearl. It is very challenging trying to understand her. I'm not sure what to do. So, I ask if she wants me to call someone. I figure if she hears family, they can keep her mind off the tube. Well, back to the twenty questions. She wants to talk to someone. I'm trying to figure out who it is. So, I'm calling out the names in the family and she will blink two times for yes. Finally, she wants me to call Yamir (Nikki's son). I realize I don't have my phone. "Pearl, I will be right back I have to go to the car to get my phone." She nods okay. I call my sister Nikki and say, "Pearl wants to talk to Yamir, I'm not sure why." Nikki says, "Oh Juice (Yamir's nickname) talked to her a lot when she is home or in the hospital." "Just have him to talk about anything." Nikki is explaining to Yamir what to do before he gets on the phone. I'm back in the room and I say, "Pearl, this is Yamir." I place him on speaker, and he is talking a mile a minute. Yamir is rambling about everything and it is nonstop. Pearl closes her eyes and falls asleep. I take Yamir off speaker, he is still talking, and then I say, "Yamir great job she is asleep, I'm going to let you go, Nikki I will call you later." It is not five good minutes and in comes the nurse, and Pearl opens her eyes. I'm thinking to myself, Jesus help, she was asleep. I say, "Pearl, I have to leave soon to go home." Pearl shakes her head no. Pearl does not like staying in the hospital by herself. As I look at the clock and it's 9:30pm, "Okay I will stay a little while longer." Pearl nods her head yes. As we watch TV, I have my hand on her hand. Then, I feel something on my head. My eyes open I look up at her and she motions for me to leave. I tell her, "I will wait until you fall asleep, I'm okay." Pearl shakes her head no and looks at the door. I reply, "I will leave in five minutes." She shakes her head no. I give her a kiss and I tell her "I will see you tomorrow love you." I kiss her on her forehead. As I'm heading towards the door, I look back and her eyes are closed. I feel better about leaving because she is resting. I call Nikki to give her a quick update. Nikki says, "Juice was crying while he was talking with Kat. Juice goes to Kat's and sit with her. And when she is in the hospital, we will call her on the phone and they would talk." I'm thinking to myself, Yamir has always brought Pearl comfort. That's something I never knew, but Pearl does and again God sends another to deliver a message. It is amazing how she wants to hear Yamir's voice only his voice. "Nikki, tell Yamir he did a great job and I'm proud of him. I'm heading home I'm tired. I'll talk with you later."

I'm driving and have about five more minutes until I reach my driveway. I do not feel well. I'm thinking my blood pressure is up and I know I need sleep. I'm home and I talk with Xavier for a few minutes, take my shower, say my prayers, and my head hits the pillow. The next morning, I figure I will not go to the hospital. I call to speak with the nurse to get an update. Pearl still needs to stay on the vent, but they are adjusting the settings which is good. I head home after work to rest. My body is speaking exhaustion, eyes burning from lack of sleep, I just can't move another inch. I can't recall the last time I had food or water and my head will not stop hurting. So, I take some Aleve. As I look at the bottle, I realize I've been taking Aleve everyday twice a day since April 2. I'm thinking, I will go to the doctor once Pearl gets better. Well the next day I head over to the hospital and Pearl is off the breathing machine. As I enter the room the first thing she says is, "I thought you were coming yesterday?" I'm thinking to myself, well she seems very salty. "Pearl, I was tired and didn't feel well so I went home to get some rest." She doesn't seem to care, as she turns her head away from me. I'm looking at her like, really? But I don't say a word. I know she has been through a lot, but I am not sure if she realizes how much we all have been through. She is mean and grouchy. I figure it's the pain, so I pay it no mind. I hug her because I am so happy to see her awake and talking, but she seems bitter. The nurse comes in and says, "Pearlie here are your meds." Pearl does not acknowledge the nurse's presences. The nurse repeats it again, "Pearlie here are your meds. Are you refusing again today?" My eyes are big, my neck goes back, and I know I have a look on my face like "SAY WHAT?" Pearl continues to look at the TV and speaks in a deep voice, "Yes." The nurse turns to me and says, "Pearlie refused medications this morning too." I ask, "Pearl, you do know what happen to you right? You know you need to take your medications to get better. So, take your meds Pearl!" Pearl is looking at the TV as if she doesn't hear me. I say again and this time the tone in my voice changes, "PEARL, are you going to take your meds?" Pearl says, "I will take' em later." I ask, "You do want to live, don't you? Let me know something, because this is not just about you." Pearl says nothing. My blood is boiling. I want to shake her so bad right now. I'm looking at her with rage and disappointment in my eyes. I'm doing everything not to speak harsh words, but she does not know what sacrifices have been made. How can someone go through all this and still be the same? I say nothing, I leave. I'm angry, crying because I am hurt. She does not care about herself, her son, mother, brothers, or the family. I'm crying because I have come to this hospital twice a day and she is not going to take her medications. Pearl is not grateful or thankful to God for what He has done. I call Vanice and say, "You take it because if she is going to do this I can't do it anymore. She is refusing to take her medications. Vanice, I'm tired, I'm done. You can have it". James is with Vanice. I'm crying, and I hear James says, "She WHAT? Oh, hell nah." I'm driving home, hitting the stern wheel. "Lord, Jesus, really, really." I'm home and I'm going for a walk. I will not go in my house with this feeling. As I'm walking, I call my mom. I need to understand why Pearl is acting this way. I'm talking, crying, and explaining. Mom is quiet, she is allowing me to get it all out of my system. I think mom is quiet because she knows I have been praying and doing what God needs for me to do for Pearl. She knows I am hurting. I also think my mom's quietness is because she is praying for her daughter and niece in this moment. "Keisha baby, you have to give it to God. You can't change Kat. God will help you and her." "Yes, ma'am.", I reply. It's amazing how my mom can say things so simple yet so powerful. I end my call and continue to walk. I realize I need to get out of my feelings and stay focus on God. The walk helps me. I'm going home, shower, pray, and sleep. Later in the week Pearl calls, I'm looking at the phone. Something is saying, "Don't answer." I know it's Pearl. I'm still a little salty, but my love for her is still here. I listen to her message and she is moving from ICU to a regular room. Now, I'm thinking is this happening again. Pearl gets better and then gives up again. She stops taking her medications, don't tell anyone anything, and then comes home despite what the doctors say. "Lord, what was this all for? What do you want me to do?"

Friday, Vanice calls me to let me know she is at the hospital and Pearl is doing better. In my mind, I am not convinced. Vanice goes on to say, "She is eating a little but not that much and she is talking some." Still, I am not convinced and I'm still a little salty at Pearl. Sunday, Vanice calls and says, "Keisha she won't eat or drink she is sleeping a lot. I feel something is coming. I'm not sure what it is." "Okay, just let her tell you what she wants. Call me if you need me, Vanice." Sunday night, I'm not feeling like myself. I can't describe it. Maybe it's because I'm not sleeping well. I'm praying still. My body is not my body. I can't place what it is, "Lord something is not right." Monday April 24th, I wake up and say, "Lord have your way with Pearl." Why did I say that? I sit up out of my sleep saying these words. I'm looking around thinking, "where is this coming from?" I'm getting ready for work and feeling like I'm floating through my morning. I'm sitting at my desk wanting to go get breakfast, but I can't move. I say, "Lord why can't I leave my desk I need something to eat?" My cell phone rings, "Keisha I need for you to get over here, Kat is back on the breathing machine and I can't understand what they are saying." It's Vanice's voice and I hear what she is saying, but I can't move. "Keisha, Keisha. Baby I don't know what is happening." "Okay, I will call over to the nurse and I will be there." I hang up with Vanice and call the nursing station. Clearly, they are not aware of what is going on in Pearl's room because they are sending the call to Pearl's nurse. I respond, "Excuse me this is." The nurse replies, "I can't talk to you I'm working on your cousin." How did she know it was me? She hangs up the phone. I jump up from my desk and I see Shay and I'm telling her. Shay says, "Go, you have to go over there." I'm looking at her and shaking my head no. "I don't want to I feel like this is not going to be good, I don't want to go." "LaQuisha, LaQuisha, go, go." I'm running through the hallway. I see someone walking beside me, gets on the elevator with me, and walks me out to my car. It's Ms. Helen McAuley. She went to high school with my mom and we have worked together for ten years. I can't look at Ms. Helen. I can't tell her what is happening because I don't want to cry. I don't have time to be in my feelings because Pearl and Vanice needs me. All I can say is "Pray, please just pray."

When I arrive at the hospital and enter Pearl's room, my eyes fill with tears, my mouth drops open, and I can't believe what I'm seeing. I turn to Vanice and she is in tears. She can't understand why this is happening again. The doctor comes in and says to Vanice, "Ma'am we need to know what are your goals for Pearl? She is back on the vent for the second time, what do you want to do because her organs are failing and there isn't anything we can do." Vanice turns to me and says, "What does she mean?" As a social worker, I know what the doctor is asking, but as Pearl's cousin and Vanice's niece I can't verbalize to my aunt what the doctor is asking. So, I turn to Vanice and say, "They need to know if you want to let her...." I stop because in this moment with tears in my eyes, I can't finish the sentence. I can't say the words. The pause isn't long, but it feels long. A lump is in my throat, my heart is shredding piece by piece because how can I ask my aunt if she wants to remove her daughter from the breathing machine? My heart, Lord, my heart it aches for Vanice, Lord I need you more now than before. Lord, help me to speak your words and not my own. Jesus intervene please. Vanice replies, "Let her go, you mean let her go, right Keisha?" I can only nod my head yes as I look her in her eyes with tears running down my cheeks. The doctor's head drops, and the nurse turns away. No one, regardless how much you hear it or must say it, no one is ready to hear a mother speak these words. It is heart breaking to see and to hear. I say to Vanice, "At any point or time, did Pearl ever say what she wanted?" Vanice states, "I was going to ask her this morning, but she got sick so fast, things happened so fast. She started last night Kat said, "Mama why are the dead bodies over there?" I said, "Kat that is not a dead body that is an air mattress." She said, "Mama that nurse said I was going to die." I said, "Kat no she didn't she didn't say that. Keisha, I don't know because I don't want anybody to be mad at me." This is when I thought back to April 2nd, when Pearl was talking to Tasha and she said, "They said I wasn't going to make it and I didn't look right." It brings chills to my body. I'm thinking Pearl knew all this time. I say, "Vanice, Pearl is your child, you have been here for her, this is not about them it's about Pearl. You have been here for her more than anyone." Vanice says, "If I just knew what to do, I have to call Tykerius, James, and Jerry. Keisha, I just don't know what to do". Then there is a knock at the door.

Chapter Four: You Know My Name

There's something about a knock that can send chills down your spine. When the unexpected is happening, there is a pause. Depending upon the situation, determines how you respond. However, in a time such as this our mouths drop, heart rates speed up, our hearing seems distant, while everything seems to slow down. The knock, it sounds meaningful. Is it the answer we've been waiting for, is it the answer we don't want to hear, or is it an answer we never saw coming? A woman enters and speaks, "My name is Beth, I'm with palliative care." As a social worker, I'm thinking what is she doing in here, palliative care is not what Pearl needs right now. I'm just going to hold my mule. Beth continues to say, "We have been working with Pearlie for a week now and the doctors thought it would be a good idea for me to come in." As she asks us to sit down, I'm looking at Vanice like "Why didn't you tell me she was seeing a palliative care social worker?" As Vanice is staring back at me like, "Who in the hell is this and what in the hell is palliative care?" Beth, says, "Our palliative care staff has been working with Pearlie since last week. She did not want us to give anyone a call, which makes our jobs difficult when this happens. However, we must respect our patient's decisions. We were going to get paperwork started, but we came in today and heard what happened." Beth turns to my aunt and says, "Mom Pearlie knew she was not going to make it out of here. She did not want to tell you because she didn't want you to worry. She was tired. She didn't tell you because she didn't want you to hurt. She didn't want you to have to make this decision if she was placed on life support again." Vanice's shoulders goes from her neck to her feet with a sigh of relief. The pressure is not on her, Vanice did not want to make the decision and now she does not have to. Beth turns to me, she utters, "Keisha, Pearlie spoke a lot about you. She thought very highly of you." Then in the moment of Beth speaking, my heart starts racing. There is a moment that it slows down. Something is about to occur and I'm not sure what it is. Beth continues, "She wanted you to make the final decision if she went back on life support." It is the answer I did not see coming. Or did I? I take in a small breath out of shock. Then I give a very small smile, nod my head yes." I realize God needed Pearl to stay a little while longer, so she could have her last moments with Him and her mother. Pearl had her mind made up. She did not want to verbalize it to us. She did not want us to hurt anymore. I can only imagine her saying "Don't tell them because they will try to convince me to fight and I'm tired of fighting." I can see her face and hear her voice. I can see her trying to fight if the right person asked her to, but I feel there is no need to fight God's plan. This makes me wonder how much courage does it take for someone to have the will to live, what about the will to die?

    The Holy Spirit speaks through me "Tomorrow at 11am we will take her off life support." There were no tears, I can't cry now. I realize God and Pearl know I can do this, but I know I can't do it in my own strength. I turn to Vanice, "Pearl is hurting, we don't want her to suffer anymore. We must let God's will be done." As she replies, "Yes," as tears fall from her face. Vanice is losing her only daughter, her baby girl. As a mother, I don't want to know how this feels and can not imagine how Vanice is feeling. She saw Pearl into the world and now has to see her leave it. There is nothing I can do for my aunt but hug her and let her know God is with us and I'm here if she needs me. I call James and Tasha to let them know what happen. They agree not to let her suffer. James will call Jerry, but we need help with Tykerius. Her one and only child. How can we tell him tomorrow may be the last day he will see his mother? Then the Holy Spirit speaks again. Beth turns to Vanice and I to ask, "Is there anything I can do to help?" I'm thinking as I'm standing looking at her. God knows your weaknesses and strengthens. All we need to do is ask and He will show up. I reply, "Tykerius, her son, will not take this well and it's so understanable. We need your help to explain to him what is going on and what will happen tomorrow." Beth motions for us to follow her and we walk into a conference room. She dials his number and say, "Hello may I speak with Tykerius please?" As she introduces herself to Ty, he politely says, "Yes ma'am, this is Tykerius." Beth starts to explain to Ty what transpired this morning. He is angry at first. Ty says, "I just want y'all to do your job and help my mom!" Ty repeated this about three times and then God uses Beth to help Ty see there is nothing else to do, but let Pearl go. Ty is listening, he is calming down and he politely says, "Yes ma'am." We can hear the cry in his voice, it's heartbreaking. It is one of the hardest things I've had to listen to. As I reflect, as a social worker, I can handle this, but I'm not a social worker right now. This is my family. This is Pearl. We grew up together, loved, laughed, cried all together. It's heartbreaking and paralyzing. As Beth ends the call with Ty, I believe Vanice and I both let out a sigh of relief. I begin calling as many people as I can while Vanice calls Pearl's dad and family. Vanice decides to stay with Pearl while I head home to talk with Xavier and mom. It is hard to deliver this news, tears and heads will drop as hearts will break.

I am home and talking with Xavier. We cry together. No questions of "why," just tears. I give him his moment and just sit with him holding him rocking him. My son is hurting and there is nothing I can do to console him. There is nothing I can do to touch the degree of pain he is feeling. All I can do is pray. As I am rocking him, I'm praying. As I wipe his tears from his eyes I'm praying. After a while, we talk about Ty. I ask if he wants to be there for Tykerius. My son being my son says, "Yes ma'am". I tell him he does not have to go in to see Pearl, just be there for Ty. I call my sister Chris to let her know and to see if my oldest nephew, Dontez wants to be there for Ty. She agrees, and he does too. When the night falls, I don't feel uneasy. I feel peace and calmness. The strangest thing is, I'm drinking water and realizing I haven't had anything to eat or drink all day. I can't remember the last time I did, but it isn't where my focus is right now.

I'm not sure when I got into the car, but I realize a decision such as this would cause me to run for the hills years ago. Years ago, I wasn't as connected with God as I am right now. I can hear Grandma saying, "Don't worry about the mule going blind, just sit back in the wagon and hold the line". Keisha don't cry yourself sick." As I look around, I'm looking for Ma. She isn't here physically to comfort me, or to hold us. What she did teach us was to stick together and to depend on each other. Ma never cried until it was all over. I know somebody must bear the cross. "Lord I'm getting stronger, but You and I both know I haven't reached that point yet. My faith is getting stronger, and my relationship with You is growing better. Still, Lord we both know I have some ways to go." I am in my car at a gas station. The ironic thing is, I'm not getting gas. I'm not getting out the car. I'm sitting and looking out the window up to the sky. I call Shay to give her the news. Shay asks, "Quisha are you sure this is what you want to do? Is there anything that can be done?" I say, "This is the right thing she is suffering and there is nothing else they can do. She wanted me to make the decision and I can't let her suffer anymore." Shay asks, "How do you feel, how are you?" I'm thinking, and I know that wasn't the first time someone asked me that, but it is the first time it registered. I respond to Shay, "I'm okay." As I end the call, I don't know what more to do but just sit. I can't believe I'm at this point in my life. I know it's happening, but it doesn't feel real. Is this peace or am I numb to what is destined to happen? I'm closing my eyes just to see when I open them if this is all a big dream. As I open my eyes, I am still here in my car at the gas station not getting gas.

*You see my eyes have closed for the last time
But I can see more than ever before
It's time it's time for my spirit to shine
So please, please don't cry no more*

Chapter Five: I'm Free

April 25th, I'm up singing "I am free." I'm not a singer only in the shower or the privacy of my own car. My voice is getting louder. The more I hear the song in my head, the louder I sing. I am smiling and singing while tears are falling down my face. It is a freeing moment for Pearl, it is a freeing moment for me. God is letting me know Pearl is free. As Xavier and I get ready, we pray and head to pick up mom. The ride is quiet. I'm praying in my head, "We need you in the rooms of the hospital. We need your peace and love to fill the rooms. No confusion or chaos to come to us, with us, or around us. Lord have your way with all of us and help everyone to see this is not about them it's about Pearl, Tykerius, Vanice, James, Jerry, and Cleveland (Pearl's dad), most of all it's about you God." Once we arrive, I go see about Vanice as she sits in Pearl's room. Mom and I walk in. This is mom's first-time seeing Pearl since she's been here. Mom looks at Pearl and then she walks out with tears rolling down her face. I need to go to her, but I'm trying to see how Vanice is doing. There needs to be more people here to help. Vanice says she is fine, but I know differently. I go over to Pearl's bed and whisper, "It's me Pearl, it's Keisha. It's going to be okay. It's going to be just fine. People are going to come in and say their goodbye's all you have to do is listen. I love you Pearl." I kiss her on her forehead. I go to the nursing station to let the nurses know I'm in the waiting room with family and will return. As I enter, I hear someone say, "Tykerius is not coming." I don't think this is a good idea. So, I ask someone to call him and be sure he doesn't want to come. The last thing I don't want is for Pearl to be removed from the vent and Ty is on his way and doesn't get the opportunity to say goodbye to his mother. Vanice calls and he says, "No, I don't want to come!" Again, I don't like the way this sounds and I'm not at ease with the idea, but I don't want to push. This is the Holy Spirit letting me know something isn't aligned with God's plan. I focus on God so while family is coming and waiting in the waiting room, I say, "You can come back to see Pearl, just not all at once." Everyone is looking at each other and trying to decide who is going back first. I'm leaving to go back in Pearl's room. I have Pandora on the gospel station, and I sit quietly as others come in to say goodbye. Tasha is by her side and she can't stop crying. Oh, they were like sisters more than cousins. "Lord, help her because I can't begin to touch the pain she is feeling and if I try Lord, I will not be able to do what you want me to do." I go over to her to say, "Tasha take a break go get some water or fresh air", but she shakes her head no. I tell her "I love you and I'm right behind you." I feel myself tearing up and now is not the time. Tasha needs to do whatever she needs to do to get her through this moment and I will sit here and be here just in case. Then a familiar face comes to the door, it is Beth. She asks how I am doing and lets me know that today, I am going to be a family member and not a social worker. Today, I am going to receive the help I give to others. Today, it is about us and not about anyone else. These are the things I would say to a family, it doesn't feel good to hear it said to me because it means we are losing someone we love dearly. I tell Beth Tykerius isn't coming and I don't feel comfortable with it. So, we go into the conference room and she calls him. He recognizes her voice, she is so good at keeping him calm. So much so, Ty decides to come and see his mother for what we know may be the last time.

    We wait for Ty to arrive. I go out to the waiting room to check on everyone. I tell them that a chaplain will come to pray with us all and if there is anyone who wants to see Pearl they can. I felt like the only one who should be in the room when she is removed from the vent is Vanice, Ty, James, Jerry, and Cleveland. I think it will be better for Pearl, but the Holy Spirit convicts me. This is hard on everyone and we all need each other. So, I say, "Anyone who wants to stay while they take her off the vent can do so." Who am I to try to take that away from anyone? God is her protector, I'm just a vessel. As they all talk among themselves, I go back into the conference room. Hours later, family comes to tell me that Ty has arrived. I run to Pearl's room trying to meet him before he enters. The first time she was placed on life support he punched the wall. I feel his emotions are going to be all over the place. I continue to pray that the Lord covers and keeps him during this time. I pray Ty will not look at me and think I'm taking his mother from him. These are my thoughts, I feel he will never want to see or speak to me again in life. I realize this is not about me but God's will. As I enter the room, he looks at his mother with tears in his eyes. Ty is 18 years old. He falls to the floor in tears. We take him out and walk him to the conference room. Vanice and I are trying to get him to calm down. Xavier, Dontez, and family from Pearl's dad side comes to the waiting room to be with him. Still no one can console him. He needs and wants his mother. There is no one who can fill this void but God. I need to step aside. I need to find somewhere quiet for a few minutes. I move into the back hallway no one is walking, talking, or present. I close my eyes, "God, please help him. Please calm and comfort him Lord. Lord, we need you Jesus please help us. We can't do this alone." I hear Ty crying as I walk back into the conference room. I see all the other young men. I watch my son and my nephew fall to the floor with tears, "Lord please," these are all young men, but in my eyes still babies, "they are hurting and there is nothing I can do to touch the degree of pain they feel." Family members are coming in and I move aside so they can all comfort each other. To have a room full of young souls grieving it's like having your heart pulled out of your chest. I'm sure through God's eyes it is beautiful to see them comforting and consoling each other.

As the cries decline, Ty stands up with a look of rage in his eyes. He goes to swing, but we stop him just before he hits the wall for the second time. His great uncle Earl is on the phone. We are not sure what he is saying to Ty but it's working. Ty decides to go back into Pearl's room. There are a few behind him. I'm moving, but just not fast enough. I'm watching Ty through the window of Pearl's room. Ty stands in the doorway, his fist tight, tears rolling down his face, and he drops again. Jerry walks him out and says, "I got you nephew, hold on to me I got you." The doctors pull me aside to let me know, she is dying on life support. It is time to remove her from the machine. I feel uneasy now. Seeing Ty, I am not able to focus. I see a familiar face coming towards me. Beth says, "LaQuisha, I told them to give you a little more time, but…" She pauses as I'm looking at her with tears in my eyes shaking my head no. All I could do is point in Ty's direction. "LaQuisha, I was running up here to help with Tykerius, but I didn't get here in time. I'm so sorry." I'm nodding my head, but I know what needs to happen. The family comes together in the waiting room for prayer and then those who want to go back to Pearl's room do so. Beth tries to prepare everyone before entering the room. "She can pass right away, it can take time, she may make noises, she may not, her breathing will change, and at the end her color will come back to what it was before." The chaplain prays while the doctor removes the machine. Pearl opens her eyes they are straight ahead, she takes a loud breath outward. The noise makes everyone stop in their place. Some begin to leave as others stay. I am in the back of the room because I don't want anyone to see me cry. I need to focus on Pearl and see her through this as well as Vanice. James, Jerry, Ty, and Cleveland decide not to come in. It's all women in the room. Then it happens, her big breath, I walk quickly from the back to her side. I tell her, "It's okay Pearl, it's okay." She continues to breathe deeply, she calls out "Mama." Beth walks Vanice up to the bed and places a wet cloth in Vanice's hand to wipe Pearl's forehead. Vanice is watching her only daughter, her baby girl leave this world. Vanice finishes and walks out quickly in tears, others leave right after. The machines start to sound. Pearl takes in a deep breath and when she did, so did I. As I stand beside her, tears rolling down my face. I'm rubbing her head, telling her, "We are here just close your eyes, we are here." My mom is beside me holding on to me. Pearl's aunt stands on the other side of the bed and everyone else is at the foot of her bed. Then the door opens, we all turn, and it is Ty. As we turn to him, every woman in this room wants to take his pain away. Every woman in this room wants to shield him from what is happening right before our eyes. I'm thinking to myself, "Lord, Lord, Jesus help!" Ty cries out "NO, NO" in a deep manly but childlike voice. His cry is a heart-breaking cry. His cry rips at your skin. He is crying out for his mother. We can't stop what God has in motion. We can't turn back the hands of time. Pearl is breathing deeply Ty is crying harder, my mom grabs him and walks him out. Pearl's aunt looks at me and shakes her head to let me know it was over. I lean in to close her eyes, but they will not close. As her aunt walks out, I realize this isn't it. Pearl heart is still beating. Before the process started, the doctor said she will come back in at the end. The doctor isn't here she is still at the nursing station looking at the monitor. I look down at Pearl and then I look up. There is only a few of us left. I see my sister Chris come in. My baby sister Nikki is beside me. I see the doctor walking in. I begin singing I am Free.

As I sing, the doctor is checking for a pulse. As she looks up she calls the time of death. Vanice comes in and I stop. She is looking at us all, no words, just looking. She turns to me and says, "No Keisha! Kat, baby no, baby why, baby why?" All the women are in the room hearts are heavy for Vanice. There is nothing we can do to touch the pain she feels. A mother standing, looking down at her child lifeless. It is a paralyzing moment. Family takes Vanice out of the room. I turn to Pearl and her color comes back. It is amazing how peaceful she looks. It is amazing how she looks like herself. It is God who is so amazing. Pearl's sister-in-law Beulah turns to me crying and says, "I can't believe this is happening, what am I going to tell my kids, what am I going to tell my kids?" I can't give her an answer because I can't speak. No one has any words we are all looking at each other with tears rolling down our faces. Beulah, Nikki,

Chris, and I look back at Pearl and just stare. Beulah leaves the room. I walk over to wipe Pearl's face and neck. Nikki and Chris stay and I start singing one more time. Nikki and I rock back and forth as we lean on each other. It is bitter sweet. You never want to see a loved one go, but you never want them to suffer. Her pain ends today. She is no longer suffering, no longer fighting a battle for her family. She is advancing to her Heavenly Father and family. In Heaven many wait for her, grandma Catherine, grandpa Bo, uncle Poboy, cousin James Brown and Uriah, nephew James Jr, her grandma Pearl, grandpa Biddy, cousin Pete and many more. Here on earth, her family remains to find a way to get through it. To search for the reasons why, to miss her, to be grateful to God, and to try to move forward with a void that only God can fill. In this moment, this is for me to see just how strong I am. It is also for me to see that death does hurt but it is also freeing. I moved out of God's way as I watched Pearl take her last breath. I watched God work with my very eyes. Before she took her last breath, I believe God freed us both. I was bound in fear of death.

Death scared me, consumed my heart, drained my spirit, and blocked my happiness to love. I realize God freed me too. I lost many when I was younger each year of my high school years. Ninth grade my uncle Poboy (William Lee Martin Jr) died in his bed. It was the very bed I slept in for the remainder of my high school and college years. Tenth grade, my cousin Nathan (Nate). I cooked for him and Poboy. Nate came to see me play basketball. I knew he was proud of me. Eleventh grade year, it was my cousin James brown (Jimmy Lee Martin Jr). One Sunday while in church, we were told he was dead in his apartment. I didn't look at church the same again for a very long time. Then my senior year, my grandpa Bo (William Lee Martin). He was the man who drove me to school and hit every trashcan there was on the side of the road. It's funny now, but not when you are eight years old. He had my snacks on the arm of his recliner as he waited for me to come from school. Then my grandmother Catherine Jane Martin everyone called her Ma or grandma. She died November 27, 2012, five days after Thanksgiving. I knew something was wrong because that Thanksgiving I went to kiss her goodbye and I said, "Love you." The surprise was she said, "I love you too." Ma never said I love you, she would just say, "Umhum." She died at home. I remember I couldn't get from Charlotte to Mt. Gilead fast enough. The last time I saw Ma, she was in a body bag. They kept her at the house until I got there. As the man unzipped the black dull body bag from her head down to her neck, I looked at her for the last time in disbelief. Her face did not look like her own. I never saw it coming. I never saw any of it coming. I took death very hard. Death took away my loved ones. It gave me a pain that no one could touch. It placed voids in my heart that no one could fill. It left me alone when everyone was around. I felt lost, abandoned, betrayed, let-down, and broken.

    Now today on April 25th, God shows me many things. He shows me I can trust in Him, to lean on His understanding and not my own. He shows me what courageous looks like. What faith looks like. Death is a painful event, but it is a part of life. I don't need to be afraid of it anymore. I know death will come again. I know He will see me through it again. I know without Him I can't do it on my own. God's plan for me, Pearl knew. She knew all this time. God had to reveal it to me in His time because I would've missed it if it was any other way. As we leave the hospital, we are all numb. We saw it happen, but we are saying to ourselves "Kat is dead, Pearl is dead." It still doesn't sound right. It's going to take time to process. On the ride home I'm driving, but I feel like I am floating. My head and heart hurts. Mom and Xavier are in the car not saying a word. Mom wants her time alone. Xavier and I head back to the house. I am not feeling well my head is still hurting, but something is different, something is wrong. I'm just not sure what it is. I know tomorrow I will need to help Vanice and the twins with arrangements. Therefore, I am going to take some Aleve, get a shower, and head to bed.

    The next day Vanice calls and say, "Keisha, Ty didn't know Kat died." My mouth drops, my heart hits the floor. "Oh my God, how did we not tell him. Where was he? Vanice are you sure? I thought he was in there. Wait he was in the room, he came in the room. Let me call James." "Why didn't someone tell Ty about Pearl?" James says, "What I told ma, Ty is in denial Keisha, we told him." "Okay, I'm going to call him now, love you, bye." The phone keeps ringing. I call back it's ringing. I'm thinking Ty pick up the phone. I hang up, I'm looking around and finally I stop. I can't do anything but pray. My head is still hurting. Later, I call Vanice to be sure to let everyone know to be at the funeral home on time.

    As I'm driving, I realize I haven't been to my hometown since my grandfather John L's (my dad's father) funeral. I feel strange still not sure what's wrong but just don't feel right. I can't describe it, but I'm just not myself. As usual, no one is ever on time. How is it I'm an hour and a half away from this funeral home, but my family is only fifteen minutes away and they are not here? I enter the funeral home and wait for everyone to arrive. Finally, Vanice, James, Jerry, Tasha, and Jasmine (Pearl's half-sister) all arrive. We are talking to the funeral home director, I realize my task maybe over. I believe what God wanted me to do was finished on April 25th. This is not what God wants of me. The meeting is over, I pull Vanice aside and say, "If you need me call, but the family can help with the arrangements. I'm going home to get some rest, I'm tired." The remainder of the night I'm in the bed not sleeping just looking at TV. The next day, my body is just slow with movement. I feel like I am walking in quick sand. I want to move, but I'm struggling tremendously to place one foot in front of the other. Later, I'm driving Xavier to AAU practice. During practice I see something in Xavier I've never seen. I'm not going to say anything right now, but I'm thinking "What is going on with Xavier?" Practice is over, and Xavier is in his feelings I can see it on his face. We are heading to the car and I say, "Xavier, why are you so upset about the call coach made in practice, it's just practice son?" He responses, "I'm not mad." Xavier "Yes you are, what's wrong?" We both are in our feelings of anger and frustration begins to show. We continue to get closer to home, it's quiet. Xavier is not wanting to talk. As I continue to drive, I'm upset because Xavier will not talk. I'm tired, I don't feel well this list goes on. I get out the car, go into the room and scream as I hit the wall. We are feeling the pains of Pearl's death, but we're trying not to. As I calm down, I go to Xavier and say, "Son what we are going through hurts. It makes you angry, sad, it's confusing and so much more, but it's better to let it out." Xavier replies, "I'm hurting mom, it's so much that's going on and I just don't know what to do," I'm sitting here with my son in my arms, I don't know what to do. All I can do is rock him as his head is on my shoulders and we are side by side. As we cry in each other arms what I don't realize is, I need to listen to myself. We sit for a while and he decides to lie down. I give him a hug and tell him to get some rest. I decide to clean a little. I start in the kitchen just to wash the dishes. Next, I start a load of clothes. Then it happens, my body is barely moving. I'm getting slower and slower. I'm trying to move but I just can't. I'm so nervous, "Lord, I know you will not bring me this far to leave me now. But Lord what's going on?" I'm walking in the dining room to sit down. I'm reminding myself, "I'm okay, to calm down". The more I said it, the better I feel, and my heart beat starts to slow down. My head, it's swimming I feel dizzy like I'm going to drop at any second. "Lord, please my son is in his room." The phone rings, it's Vanice and she is talking a mile a minute. "Keisha, the funeral home just called. They need to change some things and I just don't know what to do!" "Ok, who did you speak with and give me the number?" As I'm speaking with the funeral home director, he tries to be as gentle as possible, but I just need it direct because I don't feel well. "Please sir, just tell me the truth, please." As he tells me, I say to him calmly "I understand. I will call the family and will call you right back." I call James and luckily Jerry and Cleveland are with him. I give them the information and they agree to have a close casket and a short service. I call Vanice and she is fine with the decision. I call the funeral home director back and the task is complete. Then something says, "Okay it's time now. It's time for me to help you through this."

You see, the Lord is here, He has come to take me home
Don't worry family nothing is wrong
It's just my time, my time to go and fly with the birds
It's a feeling of peace isn't that what you've heard

Chapter Six: Let It Rain

I stand to go to Xavier's room and say, "Xavier, baby I'm not feeling well." His eyes are big, and he comes to grab me to hold me up. The look in his eyes, he doesn't need to say it I do. "I will be fine. You can stay here, you have seen a lot already. I love you son and know I will be just fine I promise so try not to worry just pray okay." I'm walking into the living room and trying to figure out who to call or text. I just can't get my thoughts together. I'm thinking what if it's nothing. It's late and I'm getting someone out of their bed to take me to the hospital. Who should I call or text? I'm in the car, I'm driving. I turn off the radio and ask God for travelling mercy. I arrive to the hospital, get out of the car, and I'm walking funny. I can't understand why I'm staggering. I haven't had a drink or anything what is really going on? I continue to walk, and I show my work badge. I know the treatment should be the same regardless, but I know it will not hurt if they know I am one of them. I'm at the desk and my arm feels strange my chest feels heavy and I can't hold myself up any longer. I give the receptionist my name and say as I hold my badge to her, "I don't feel well." She calls for a wheelchair and seconds later I drop into the wheelchair. I'm talking with the triage nurse, and I'm trying to figure out what is going on. I'm telling her about Pearl as her eyes fills with tears, I say to her "I'm fine. I know I made the right decision, I know she is no longer suffering. I was fine when I left the hospital on Tuesday, I can't figure out what is going on ma'am what is going on?" She looks at me, grabs my hand and replies, "Honey you are grieving." I say, "No you don't understand, I'm fine with what I did. I've been okay all this time, I've held it together, worked, went to see her twice a day, took my son where he needed to go, and Tuesday we took her off the vent. It was the right decision, I'm at peace." She looks at me and replies, "I understand, but your adrenaline was getting you through. I need for you to relax and let go of my arm and loosen up your left hand for me." "What are you talking about ma'am I don't have…" and I look down. In my right hand is the sleeve of her shirt. My left hand is so tight as I open it, it's red on the inside. "I'm so sorry, I'm so sorry." She utters, "Honey I need for you to calm down and breathe for me okay, we are going to take good care of you." "Please, something is wrong, I feel like I've been in a car crash. My body it's aching, I'm cold, my body it hurts so bad, why is this happening? I don't think I was in an accident." She says, "Honey your body and mind has caught up with each other and now you are grieving. Again, your adrenaline helped you through this. This is what grieving looks like." I'm thinking to myself; I have faith. Did I lose my faith? Do I not believe God's will was done? I don't understand what is happening. I was okay with the decision. I was okay when I left the hospital. I was calm. I was at peace. What happened, where did I go wrong? As I waited for the doctors, they place me in another room. I know if I'm in a quiet place I can listen for God and I will calm down. I need to get some sleep and get warm, I'm so cold why am I shaking like this. Now it's quiet, I text mom to go sit with Xavier and to get my clothes out the wash machine and place them in the dryer. There's nothing wrong with me I just needed to be still for a moment. As the nurse comes back in, my blood pressure is dropping but it's still high. Slowly it's going down, but I still can't figure out why my body is in so much pain and I'm hurting all over. The doctor comes in and he asks me questions and I answer. He asks me to touch my nose with my fingers and other things. I'm responding to his request but talking to him about Pearl. I ask, "Why is it so hard for me to lift my arm, it feels heavy?" I see him pinching me, but I don't feel much of it. I see it, but not feeling it. Again, I'm wondering why my body feels like someone beat me up and I lost badly. He replies, "Ms. Martin, I'm not sure if you are having a stroke or not, but we need to keep you here for observation." STROKE, what the!" He replies, "Your blood pressure is up." I'm thinking well your blood pressure will go up too if you are told you may be having a stroke. I immediately say to myself, calm down now. Let them do whatever, but calm down, you are not having a stroke.

"Lord please, Lord please my son and my mother are home. Lord I must take care of them Lord please help me." The triage nurse is in the room, she turns to say, "Try to open and close your hands, continue to open and close your hands." I look down my hands are closed tightly. I try but my arm feels so heavy. Later, another nurse comes in to say, "Ma'am we will be transporting you to Cabarrus." "No ma'am, I have a son I can't go to Cabarrus county." She replies, "Okay we will see if we can get you to CMC main." This is when the MESS hit the fan. I scream "No that's where my cousin died please ma'am don't' send me there please, please don't!" I grab her hand. In my head I don't know where all of this is coming from, I know I need to get myself together, but I can't. The nurse stays with me for a while. I'm thinking, why am I sounding crazy and out of control right now? The doctor orders something for me to sleep, they ask if I've been sleeping. I say, "Honestly, I don't know, I think so." Now, I'm wondering, was I sleeping? I think I was, but I just don't remember if I was truly sleeping. Before giving me medication, they find a room for me in the hospital. As they are pushing me onto the floor, I hear familiar sounds from machines. I say, "Where am I?" The nurse responds, "ICU." "Oh, no ma'am can't stay up here I have been in ICU for almost a month with my cousin I can't stay here!" I'm trying to take off the stickers and tags from the monitors. The nurse says, "Laquisha, you are dehydrated, tired, and you are grieving, but you will be just fine. You are here because this was the only bed we have available when another is available we will take you down to the next floor." I can hear myself sounding crazy, but I can't keep myself from talking crazy. I call my sister Chris to let her know what's going on. I can't recall our conversation. It seems like minutes later, but I open my eyes to someone saying, "Hello it looks like you got some pretty good sleep." I feel somewhat strange like completely out of it. My body is sore like I had been in a fight. My head still hurts. I didn't feel like myself. They are running test. I feel like I need something, but not sure what it is. Things are foggy, but I do know I'm not in ICU. I was sleeping very well. My head still hurts, I feel dizzy, and weak. My body does not feel like mine. I am present but feel completely absent from my own body. I feel a little better than before. My cell phone rings and it's Vanice. I know if I don't answer she will call back until I do. So, I try to pretend I am okay. I can't recall the full conversation. I hear "Hey baby, are you coming home?" Vanice is referring to our hometown. My response is, "Yes, I might." Then she asks, "Are you coming to the funeral?" I pause, because I don't know if I am going to be out of the hospital in time for the funeral and I don't want her to know I'm in here. I say, "I will try." I'm not sure what's prompting Vanice, but she asks, "Keisha are you in the hospital?" I sit up in the bed and slowly I say, "Don't you worry about me I will be fine. Don't tell anyone because I don't want anyone to worry, but Yes, I'm in the hospital." She says, "Your blood pressure right?" I look at the phone and I'm wondering how did she know but I say, "Yes." I'm sure she is saying more right now, but I have no idea. I'm not sure how the conversation ends. I get another call. I'm not sure of the time or what day it is. I answer the call and I hear "How are you dear?" It is Mrs. Linda and I try my best not to let on I'm in the hospital. "I reply, "I'm good, how are you?" She says, "Laquisha Martin, where are you?" I pause and say very slowly, "I'm in the hospital Mrs. Linda." Mrs. Linda is a nurse, but her connection with God, Jesus, and the Holy Spirit is strong. I'm sure the Holy Spirit guided her to call me. All I can remember is her saying, "Laquisha, honey you have to take care of yourself. Me and Mr. C love you." Mr. C (Cedric, aka Pops) is Mrs. Linda's husband. He has always treated me like his daughter, therefore I call him Pops. I know they are going to start praying as soon as she ends the call. I know I will be okay, I just need some time, my body needs some time.

    Well, I'm not sure of the things going on or what day it is. My friend, Fretral, stops by to check on me. After he leaves, I'm extremely tired so I sleep some more. I'm going down for test. I'm still feeling bizarre, swimmy head, weak, lost. I feel lost in my body. I come back up to the room and sleep. I go back down for more test. I enter the room and Jeanette and her daughter, Dannisha, are here. I'm trying to tell Jeanette everything I can remember. I tell her if anything happens to me, I have paperwork completed and she is my voice. Well it doesn't take long for that to kick in for Jeanette. The doctor comes in a few hours after my test. He is talking, but I have no idea what he is saying. I do hear Jeanette talking a mile a minute. I'm looking at her while nodding. I can't speak I'm tired. They are discharging me. I'm riding with Jeanette, while Dannisha is following with my car. We head to the pharmacy and they are closing. I need my medicine and I need it today. Jeannette jumps out the car and heads in. I'm walking as fast as my body will allow but I just don't feel good. I can't move that fast. My head is still swimming, my body is sore. The pharmacist, Brooke, is heading to a party, but after Jeanette finish talking and I reach the counter she feels badly. Brooke tilts her head to the side as I'm walking up. She fills the prescriptions. Apparently, I look like how I feel, which is like I was in a fight and lost. We are pulling up in my driveway. I'm walking into the house and I see my mom looking at me strangely, but she doesn't say anything. I don't recall seeing Xavier, but my nephew Dontez is sitting beside me and places his head on my shoulder. As I look around my living room, I see my mother standing at the door, my nephew head on my shoulder, my sisters cooking in the kitchen, Jeanette getting all my medications together, and my little nieces and nephew looking frighten. I want to jump up and say don't worry, but I'm just not able. We all have heavy hearts, we all have emotions we just can't describe. We all have been through the storm. I don't want them to leave, I want to be with my family. I can't verbalize it though. It's like I'm too tired to talk. Nikki helps me to the bed and lies with me. It brings tears to my eyes my baby sister hurting for our lost, her own lost Uriah, and worrying about me. Chris is taking care of things in my house. They make me proud. Events after this is a blur. I'm not sure what day it is. I struggle to find my way. I decide to go to the funeral. I know I should stay home but I go anyway.

After the funeral I am outside, someone asks me if I am okay. I honestly say, "no." I feel it coming on again, but what is it? My head is hurting and swimming, my arm is heavy, and I just can't get my breath but this time I am crying. I'm falling. I hear my name, I hear different voices, but I'm not sure where I am. I hear Vanice calling my name and seeing Xavier at my legs. I'm saying, "I'm okay, I'm okay" and it's pissing my mom off. She replies, "Stop saying that." I wanted to say, "I need to know I'm okay and if that makes you feel uncomfortable then leave because I'm trying to calm down!" I may be going through something but disrespecting my mom would not result in a good outcome. I'm in Jeanette's house and Xavier is on my right side. I want to jump up and yell I'm fine, but I can't get my body to move. Someone checks my blood pressure and I hear them say, "Jeanette look." There is a moment I want to high five Jeannette, but I just can't get my arm up. In my head I'm smiling, but I don't think this is the expression on my face. I want to say I'm proud of you, but I can't speak the words. Nikki comes to my side and I say, "Get Xavier out! I need for you to get him out." Someone does, but it isn't her because she stays right beside me. Nikki looks at me to reassure me I will be okay. I see her fear and I want so much to take the fear away from her. Nikki has been through a lot and I don't want to add to it. She doesn't say a word, she stands here beside me. I am scared because I can't figure out why this keeps happening? It has never happened before. All the deaths I've been through, it wasn't like this. I am trying to talk, but it is coming out slow or I just can't get it out at all. I can hear myself and it doesn't sound right. It's like I am talking to myself, but they can't hear me. Tasha comes in and whispers in my ear "What's wrong? I thought I told you to be strong?" A tear rolls down my face because I am strong, I have been doing this for a month, I'm exhausted but I can't tell her. The words won't come out of my mouth. As the paramedic is talking, Jeanette interprets, "Are you going to take her or not?" The paramedic does not respond to Jeanette, he turns to me and says, "Ma'am can you smile?" I'm not sure who ask the question, "Why are they asking her to smile?" My uncle Dan says in a deep very concern and scary voice, "To see if she is having a stroke." I hear the word STROKE, oh no not this again! I'm not having a stroke, "Lord why can't they hear me. I'm very aware of what is going on. I don't know why I can't speak. Lord, help me to speak." You know I feel like God is saying, "No, you have spoken enough, now it's time for me to use others to speak for you." Jeanette is doing just that she is my voice. I'm in the ambulance and I'm back at the hospital. It's all happening so fast. I'm not able to recall it all. I'm not sure if I was given something or not, but I feel like I'm floating. I'm in the hospital bed and feel a pop and when the pop happens, I can move my arm and neck. The nurse says, "Just hold this right here." She is taking blood. After this I'm not sure what happens. I go home from the ER, but I can't tell you how I got home or who is taking care of me.

    I know the days are very long. I have a doctor's appointment and I'm driving myself. I'm still not feeling like myself. I honestly feel like I'm having an out of body experience, but in quick sand at the same time. It's the strangest feeling.

My doctor comes in and she is on the computer. After reading, she turns to me and says, "You are grieving and what you did for your cousin was the right thing." I want to say how do you know but I just don't have the energy to ask. She writes me out of work for two weeks. I ask if I can just go back. She says, "No, you will not." I'm thinking I need to get back to what I know. Being in the house by myself for long periods of time, I'm not going to do it. My head still feels swimmy and I am just out of my zone. Can you recall going through a storm and feeling like you are by yourself? You don't have the energy to call anyone or ask for help. You are exhausted. I'm thinking if I can just get back to work, I will be okay. I want to get back to the routine I know so I can focus on my heartache/loss. I'm not sure how long it is but I'm going back to work.

    The first day back to work, I journal "Today is my first day back since Pearl was placed back on life support for the second time. Today, I'm not going to focus on that day. Today, I'm thanking you God for the ability to breathe. Thank you for a day of rejoicing in your name. Lord, you brought us to this, and you will see us through it because only You can. Lord, you are our Rock and our salvation. You have given us what we need in our own time. For that Lord, I thank you. Happiness, smiles, victory. Today we are saying THANK YOU. In the name of the Father, Son, and Holy Spirit.." I don't have many conversations, but a few people come to check on me. Tears fall from my face as they ask, "How are you?" as they give me hugs. It's nothing like someone asking you how you are after someone has died, but the hug. Why hug when it is the most sensitive time? It's for comfort but it truly reminds you of the pain. It's like when they press up against you the pain just flows out of your heart and your mind recalls death has come again. The pain reaches the surface of your heart and you try to say to yourself, "Don't cry." It's hard not to, the hug is meant to be comforting, but it hurts you emotionally. I don't want to talk but someone wants to talk about her mother passing a few years ago and how she had to explain it to her daughter. I'm thinking I feel for you really, but I truly don't want to listen to this right now. Do I say this, nope I listen? I feel like a train wreck. What was I thinking coming back to work? I want to work but this isn't a good idea, but I'm here. Finally, she leaves, and I head to my supervisor's office. I tell her what happened and say, "I am really trying not to close my door, but I don't want to see people right now." I keep my door close when something is wrong with my family, I just can't take it. It hurts badly when I can't help. It hurts now because I can't bring Pearl back, but I don't want to. So, when I'm at work I close my door. I hear God better in the quietness and I don't have to show people my pain behind closed doors. Although I'm in my office, I'm still able to hear people and it brings me comfort. Whereas at home, it's just me while Xavier is in school. Later, my phone rings, its Beth the palliative care social worker. She wants to check on us. I tell her everything. She recommends I go to grief counseling. Beth says, "Laquisha, I noticed your family depends on you a lot. I also noticed you are a social worker all the time even when you shouldn't be, I think it would be healthy for you to talk with someone." I think it's a good idea, just can't figure out how I am going to do all of this, work, take Xavier wherever he needs to go etc.... Beth says, "Laquisha, we as social workers take care of everyone else, but ourselves. It's time for you to start taking care of yourself." "I agree, Beth."

So, I call hospice and make an appointment. But I don't attend the appointment. I take Xavier to basketball training. Xavier says, "Mom go to your appointment I will be fine," but no

I take him to training. Apart of me wants to go but do not know how to do for me and not him. Is it going to hurt him if he doesn't go to training, nope not at all? I feel guilty if I don't take him but feel like I let myself down by not going. So, I reschedule. The next day I'm in my office and decide to go say hello to Shay. She asks if I am okay. I say, "Yes I guess so, I realize whenever I cry I stop myself." Shay asks, "Why?" I just can't explain. What she asks next brought tears to my eyes. "Are you upset with Pearl?" I hear her clearly, but I feel a certain type of way after she asks. At first, I ask, "Why ask me that, I'm not?" Now I'm thinking, Shay isn't the first to ask me this question. The hospice social worker asked me this when I spoke with her briefly on the phone, I just can't recall why the question is being asked. Still, I don't feel like I am upset with Pearl. I look at Shay and say, "No and start crying?" Tears will say what you can't. In this moment in the room I realize "Yes I'm upset with Pearl." Before I excuse myself, Shay replies "It's okay to cry LaQuisha and it's okay to be upset with her. It doesn't mean you don't love her, it means making a decision like that is a lot." I nod my head and excuse myself. As I head back to my office, I recall writing something at my kitchen table the night I went to the hospital. I go home; the paper is still on the table. The sheet reads "I am angry because

> 1. She left it for me to decide when to take her off the life support, but I know she trusted me that much.
>
> 2. When I asked her if she wanted to stop she said no, but she was only protecting us.
>
> 3. I thought she just didn't care anymore when she refused her medicine, but she already knew she was dying.

4. I'm just getting better from grandma's death and now I'm grieving again, but that's a part of life.

5. All the running and doing no one wonder about me, but they did.

6. We are all in different locations and not all together, but peace is a virtue

7. I knew I needed medical attention, but I put it off. I ended up going to the doctor.

8. Life continues, and I feel I'm in slow motion.

9. I'm angry and I don't want to be but it's a part of grieving.

10. I don't want to go tomorrow to feel pain but it's better to feel it with everyone instead of by myself.

11. I thought I was at peace when I left her at the hospital but I'm at peace with the decision, I can still grieve".

After reading this, I realize journaling is my outlet. I know if I get back to what I know to be the norm; I can figure out what I need to do. So, I write.

Chapter Seven: Mercy Said No

You don't really realize how much you have inside of you until you start talking about it. As a social worker, I know talking to someone helps. The first visit I missed. I'm attending the second appointment. The session is emotionally taxing. "Oh, dear Lord, how am I going to get through this. How am I going to get better? God said If you will take one step, He will take two. Lord, I must get better something is stirring in me and I'm not sure what it is." As I continue with counseling, my therapist is having me to do many exercises. I refer to myself as Laquisha and Keisha in my sessions. I realize I see myself as Keisha when I'm around my family. Keisha is the quiet girl from Mt. Gilead, NC. She cries when death comes, people consoles her because it is so overwhelming. Keisha is also loud and funny around her family. Laquisha is the single mother raising her son, social worker, friend, the responsible person. Laquisha is the grown-up version of Keisha. No, I have not lost it. I'm still sane, but everyone has the inner child in them, and Keisha is mine. The therapist wants me to get a card and sign my name. This is because I realize for whatever reason I never sign my name to a card. I feel it defines ownership of the feeling and I don't want anyone to know how I feel. Sounds strange, it is, but I own my insane moments, do you? Anyway, I decide on a card and it reads to LaQuisha:

"That day we met our paths didn't just cross, they merged together and became one. Wherever our path leads us I know it will be an amazing journey, because we're together and that's all that matters. I love you." I write on the blank side of the card "Laquisha, it has been a while and I'm very thankful that we met again. You were a part of my life for many years and because of life's accumulations, we went our separate ways. April 2, 2017, we became one again. Yes, the circumstances were of another, but it was for our own good. Laquisha you have always been a strong mother, provider, focused, kind, a prayer warrior, a woman of fairness, wanting to be alone, talking with family but not wanting to be with them. For me, I am timid, fearful, crying all the time, unsure, patient, peaceful, loving, fun, wanting to be around family. We both have endure pain, loss, loneliness, but there has been joy, laughter, happiness, love, success, and victory. When we met again, we became one. It was truly love, joy, peace, longsuffering, kindness, goodness, faithfulness, gentleness, and self control, the fruit of the Spirit (Galatians 5:22-23). God picked you for Pearl, but He knew you couldn't do it without me. So, He slowly introduced me back into your life. You didn't see it at first. The times you wanted to cry that was me, the times you wanted to be rescued, that was me. The moments you felt weak, unsure that was me. No matter how much you tried to ignore it, God continued to bring me forth in your life. He realized it was time for me to be a part of your life again. My prayer is to stay together and not depart again, but I know whatever God's will is shall be done. I wanted to say Thank You for allowing me to enter back into your life. Thank you for accepting ME for Me. Thank You for the love and reassurance that whatever we face it will be together instead of apart. Welcome back LaQuisha, I look forward to our future together." Signed Keisha.

The next card, I make for myself I place a picture of my mother and myself together and a picture of Ma, at the bottom of the page. On the front of the card it reads, "Keisha you were designed for this." The inside of the card reads

"Grandma would say, "Don't worry about the mule going blind just sit back in the wagon and hold the line. What doesn't kill you makes you stronger. Cry, but don't cry yourself sick." Mom will say, "Don't worry about it baby, just pray about it. Go into your closet and pray." I will say "Everybody wants the credit, but don't want to do the work." Keisha, you have it in you because you were designed for it all. Being weak gives you the opportunity to get stronger. Crying cleanses, the soul and brings forth a pure heart and mind. You have what it takes close your eyes and look. It's the kind that's passed down through generations hand to beautiful hand each reaching out and pulling another one through. We have you but don't be afraid to let go. We didn't get here because it was easy, but we didn't get here alone. You are just where you need to be. Breath baby girl breath. Live life and if you fall get back up. Don't be afraid to love yourself or to love others. Signed LaQuisha."

In therapy, I'm not talking about Pearl only. I'm reaching back to the deaths we had as I was growing up. The difference is I realize in my younger years I cried more. I allowed myself to feel more. Now, I don't do it as much as I need to. I feel like crying is a sign of weakness. I don't want to be seen by my family as "weak." I know I am stronger this time around. God is all over me and in me this I know. I feel my family can't say I'm still the little girl who needs consoling and watching over. I'm growing, and God is helping me. It's also good to be weak because it gives God time to strengthen me. During therapy a lot of the things I know, but just do not want to speak aloud. I MISS MY GRANDMA. It hurts because she is not here. My heart aches still. Only God and time will help this ache. I did not see her death coming at all. It was a hit to my heart I have yet to truly recover from. I find myself ignoring the fact she is gone. I'm really feeling the pain, I left behind. I'm working hard to ignore it. I was trying to ignore it, but no more. I cry, and I cry. I feel whatever I'm feeling about Pearl and grandma and I acknowledge to myself it's okay to feel this. It's okay to stay in it for a little while. As grandma would say, "Cry, but don't cry yourself sick."

The next assignment is to write to myself. When I journal I write down my thoughts. I started writing to grandma and then Pearl. This time, I'm writing to Keisha. Is this hard, yes? I feel a little strange talking to myself. My first entry reads:

"It's been a moment, but I'm glad I decided to drop in to chat. I've been setting up Xavier's schedule for the summer. God is opening doors. As for the family, I'm staying close to home right now to build up physically so that I can be strong. It took a lot out of me. Sometimes you just don't know how tired you are until you sit down. I'm slowly coming into my own. I'm different, and I realize I don't want to go back to the "old me." Yes, it hurts to see Pearl go, but it was also Peaceful and joyful to see how God carried her home. How can I be hurt about it?

God moved in so many ways. I'm smiling and grateful. I'm talking about God and how He is advancing because He is. I'm overjoyed with what He has done in me. You see I was an angry person. I would hold my feelings inside and just keep going. Well, I'm finding that saying what I need to say and not what I want to say is a big difference. Then I give it to God. It keeps the blood pressure down, less stress. I pray I will do this and not go back to my old ways. I also want to be sure I don't take on other problems. I realize I'm a "fix it" type person, but I am not God is. This goes with Xavier too. I must allow him to do and trust God and trust that God is in Him. It would be less stressful. I went to get a pedicure last Friday. I was running late, and I told the guy, "Don't worry about the time; I deserve this, so take your time." I sat there realizing I do deserve my time to relax and not stress. Keisha, it felt strange I must say. I'm truly not use to it. It felt different and out of the ordinary, but it was done. I was proud of myself. Because I usually talk myself out of doing something for just "ME!" It's time I stopped and did something for ME at least twice a month. A movie, pedicure, massage by myself. Just enjoy me. I'm finding I can't control what will happen. I know right, like I have it like that makes you laugh. Well, I just thought it was the funniest thing. Girl, you are not God, but you trust in Him. Whatever happens it happens don't be fearful of what you don't know just believe and trust in God."

Writing to myself helps me to find me again. You know it is strange at first but doing something new will feel this way. What I'm realizing in therapy is: I'm not able to fix everything and everyone, I don't like taking on other people's stuff. I neglect myself. I will spare other's feelings even if they don't spare mine. I realize I hold grudges. I realize I'm a great person, mother, daughter, sister, and friend. I realize I can be all these things, but I still need to know my limits and take time out for myself. As I continue with therapy, I realize I need to enjoy life and trust God.

So now what does the future hold? I'm not sure. I will do my very best to live life. I will be the best me God wants me to be. Death will come again, but GOD…. He will see us through it. Not the same way but He will see us through it. I realize my faith is truly built on my experiences. God is always present, but it is me who needs to find Him and enhance my relationship with Him. If you did not know Pearl, please know you missed out on a truly amazing individual. She was a blessing to have, to know, but most of all to be loved by and to have loved. I don't know what Pearl would say to us as her family and friends. However, I like to think it is something that would let us know she is just fine. I believe she is truly walking around in Heaven. I can imagine her saying this to the family.

Let's Close Our Eyes

Can you feel the peace inside of me?
I've closed my eyes and you will never imagine what I see
The clouds family the clouds are so beautiful and white
The feeling is something I will never feel twice

I've closed my eyes and you will never imagine who is holding my hand
Do you feel the peace, the peace inside of me?
It's the Lord family, I pray that you will understand
It's a feeling that no man can give but only receive

You see, the Lord is here, He has come to take me home
Don't worry family nothing is wrong
It's just my time, my time to go and fly with the birds
It's a feeling of peace isn't that what you've heard

I've closed my eyes and the song is loud and clear
I can feel Him family, I feel His presence here
He makes no mistakes, trust in Him and you will see
This is why I ask, please don't grieve for me

Family, I've closed my eyes and I can see us, I can see us in my dreams
Don't worry, we will meet again when you receive your wings
So please, please don't fight or fuss
Because in the Lord my family, we all should trust

You see my eyes have closed for the last time
But I can see more than ever before
It's time it's time for my spirit to shine
So please, please don't cry no more

You see, I closed my eyes and He, The Lord is here like Ma said
If it's too hard, please bow your heads

I feel no pain the worries are gone, and I am at peace
So, now can you see Family, can you feel that your Pearly Pearl is FREE.
Family, just close your eyes

Written by LaQuisha "Keisha" Martin

Thank You God

God, Jesus, and the Holy Spirit words can't explain the magnitude of my thanks. This journey was designed by You, Almighty God. I knew it was You in my times of doubt, fear, even reassurance. The Holy Spirit helped me to realize it was YOU and You were always there. "So do not fear, for I am with you do not be dismayed for I am your God. I will strengthen you and help you; I will uphold you with my righteous right hand" (Isaiah 41:10).

"Then Jesus told them you are going to have light just a little while longer. Walk while you have the light, before darkness overtakes you. Whoever walks in the dark does not know where they are going. Believe in the light while you have the light, so that you may become children of light. When he had finished speaking Jesus left and hid himself from them" (John 12: 35-36).

When I began to worry you said, "Do not be anxious about anything, but in everything by prayer and petition with thanksgiving present your requests to God. And the peace of God, which transcends all understanding will guard your hearts and your minds in Christ Jesus" (Philippians 4:6-7).

When I became weary and troubled, You said: "Do not let your hearts be troubled. You believe in God believe also in me. My Father's house has many rooms if that were not so, would I have told you that I am going to prepare a place for you? And if I go and prepare a place for you, I will come back and take you to be with me that you also may be where I am. You know the way to the place where I am going". (John 14:1-4).

Special Thanks

Xavier, "He gives strength to the weary and increased the power of the weak. Even youths grow tired and weary, and young men stumble and fall; will renew their strength. They will soar on wings like eagles; they will run and not grow weary, they will walk and not be faint" (Isaiah 40:29-31). Son, I will always thank God for you. I truly saw how God has moved in you more during this time than ever before. Xavier, you allowed God to speak through you to guide you. You truly held on to God when times were rough, and I am so very proud of God in you. He is advancing son, and I know God is not done with you yet. Love you.

Bernice Martin my mother who will say "just go into your closet baby and pray about it". I thank you for before, present, and what's to come. I listened mama all those years you talked about God and you thought I was just looking out the window. I was listening. Look how God advanced mama. Look at who you raised. I thank God for you, love you.

Chris and Nikki Martin my dear sweet strong sisters. You both were there when I needed to let out my frustration. You were there when I needed to be weak. You both were there in different ways, but you both were there. God spoke to you both and you listened. He used both of you and it was displayed beautifully. Thank you both love you both.

Jeanette Martin-Green one of my oldest cousins but more like my oldest sister. I truly cannot say with words how I feel about you. I remember Pearl saying, "Kay told me Jeanette was your ride or die chick and no one better not stress her out or they had to deal with you Keisha". I said it, you are that woman, you are that ride or die chick for me. You didn't say much but you were right there physically by my side. I knew I could do it but when I wasn't able to you were right there. I love you and thank God for you.

Martin Family thank you all for being there for each other It has been a long five years, but God is still own the throne. Ma raised us right. If we did not do anything for each other, we are always there when we are in need. She raised us this way and I know she looked down at us saying, "well done". We did what we were to do, and we did it with God and there is no one better to go through a storm with but God. When times get hard, go to your closet and pray about it, cry but don't cry yourself sick. Remember to live life to the fullest.

Shay Phillips, you are truly a great friend. Each time I came to you about Pearl, it was always, the Holy Spirit guiding your words. Your medical knowledge was always beneficial and informative. It was God in you that I have found to be so beautifully profound. It's so easy to see God in you dwelling around you. I'm forever grateful to God for you.

Mrs. Linda Elder, they say people come into your life for a reason, season, or lifetime. I don't know God's plans for us but we have truly held strong for each other. It's amazing how my mind would drift/float and you would text or call with your sweet angelic voice and say only how you can say it, "how are you dear"? You will never know how much I appreciate and admire you. You are truly filled with the Holy Spirit. I see and hear it every time we have conservations. I thank God for you.

Mr. Cedric Elder (Pops), thank you for the prayers and although we send messages through Mrs. Linda, you have always been a tremendous blessing. You have always made me feel like a daughter and I'm so very grateful. I thank God for you.

Joann Graham, our friendship has grown over the years. I must say God used you in a way that I will never forget. He continues to use us both because we talk about God so much now. God has plans for us, you will see. Thank you for just being you Jo. Love you my friend.

Bethany Link, I prayed for an understanding supervisor after Will Fields left. I waited and prayed and prayed and waited. I didn't realize the reason I was praying this prayer was because of this. Oh, I never saw this coming, but throughout it all you never questioned, you never turned me away. You always stopped and gave me the time and attention needed. You reminded me to take care of myself when my focus was on Pearl and my family. I'm so forever grateful for you. Thank you for allowing the Holy Spirit to lead you.

Dr. Rhonnie Song, God had you in perfect alignment because you truly were His vessel in my life during those lonely moments in the hospital. The nonverbal gestures were Heaven sent and it will never go without recognition or appreciation. I thank God for you and thank you for being obedient to God to help me during my time of need.

Dr. Darin Kennedy, I want to say thank you for taking the time out to give me ideas on how to write a book. You always stopped what you were doing to give me your advice. For that, I'm truly grateful.

Dr. Tayo Adentunji, I want to say thank you for the encouragement. Thank you for the talks in my office that reminded me God is still in it all. Most of all, thank you for believing in me and reminding me, I can do it. Love you

Fretral McRae, we have been friends for many moons. This go around my friend you truly stepped up in a mighty way. Thank you for the visits to the hospital and taking Xavier and my mom to and from where they needed to go. You didn't say much and that was truly okay. It was the actions, which spoke loudly. You had my family and me at the forefront of your mind and for that, I'm so grateful. Love you my friend.

To everyone else doctors, nurses, social workers and anyone else who I may not mention by name, I want to say thank you for the support and guidance through this time. May God Bless you all.

Catherine Jane Martin "Ma", I saved the best for last. I know you are looking down and saying, "umm huh." You were a woman of few words when it came to emotions, but you displayed your love in so many ways. There are no words that can bring forth the amount of love, gratitude, respect, and the honor it was to have you in my life. All the times I cried on your shoulders, you fixed my scrapes and scratches, the laughs, food, and fun. I remember the moments with Grandma Virginia. The three musketeers we were. We sat on Grandma Virginia's porch for hours. Grandma Virginia would say, "Keisha baby don't go behind them bushes with the little boys". For a long time, I did not know what that meant, but I never went behind the bushes with little or big boys. I remember all the special saying you would say like, "Don't worry about the mule going blind. Just sit back in the wagon and hold the line. Cry, but don't cry yourself sick. My favorite saying that would stop a person in their tracks is, "Speak when spoken to. Come when you're called. You will make someone a good old house dog". Yes, ma'am that one is cut throat in your face type of comment. Don't worry, I don't use it. You were our rock and you still are. We love you, miss you, but will not pray you back to this world. Can you believe how God has changed me? Can you believe all that He has done in me? Would you ever think Grandma I could do this? I know what you are saying, "Keisha, you can do all things through Christ who strengthens you".

About the Author

I am LaQuisha Martin. My family calls me Keisha. I'm a proud mother to Xavier. A daughter to Bernice Martin and Bruno Green. A sister to Christal and Nikki Martin and Omar Green. I was born in Mount Gilead, NC. I was raised by my maternal grandparents Catherine and Bo Martin, while my mom worked very hard in hosiery and lumber mills/factories. I attended UNC-Charlotte and received my bachelor's degree in Psychology and Sociology and minor in Gerontology. I later completed my Master's in Gerontology. I'm currently a Social Worker in the health care field for eleven years.

God brought me to a place of freedom. My heart was once paralyzed to experience death of my loved ones. Death placed me in a state of helplessness and hopelessness. This storm freed me from the very thing that paralyzed me. God made death victorious for Pearl and me. Through this experience, my faith enhanced. My relationship with God is profound. I will be able to look back and pull from this moment for what is to come. I know death will come again. I know death is a part of life but is beautiful to see when God is present. I have my moments, but my moments don't have me anymore. With Pearl, I saw how much courage it takes for the "will to live" and the "will to die".

www.ingramcontent.com/pod-product-compliance
Lightning Source LLC
Chambersburg PA
CBHW031422160426
43196CB00008B/1013